Praise for *Who am I Today?*

"Raw, authentic voices of women and their snapshots of their journeys. Makes us realize we all have so much within us to share that can resonate profoundly with others; it truly behooves us all to put pen to paper and expose ourselves. As we see/read, it all flows in a most self-reflective and poignant style."

> ~ Harriet Cabelly, LCSW, author of *Living Well Despite Adversity: Inspiration for Finding Renewed Meaning and Joy in Your Life*

"This successful anthology engages readers from start to finish in a first read, and sends the reader back to favorites many times. Jennifer Minotti has inspired writers with a simple question that evokes authenticity and generates captivating stories. The answers to *Who Am I Today?* are as fresh and diverse as the contributors who share them. This collection throbs with awakening in the midst of illness, fierce self-love in the face of abuse, and sexy toughness after the loss of a spouse. The brave truths, shared in prose and poetry, tease out our own answers. In the words of one writer, 'I refuse to waste time at war with what is ... I want words to be bridges instead of weapons.' Minotti's project convinces us, in every selection, that the act of writing, itself, is an answer."

> ~ Kelly DuMar, author of *girl in tree bark*

"*Who Am I Today* is a testament to women's perseverance, vulnerability and their ability to transform, especially when confronted with the darkness within. The anthology shines light on how it feels to look inward, what it means to slowly slide into the perspective of inner truth, and what it's like to discard self-judgment induced by those confining social standards—and to simply look, open one's eyes and see that fountain of inner power. Women from various backgrounds and different countries ask themselves this trick question, *'Who Am I Today?'* The answer to what we all, as collective consciousness need to feel and identify with, and to find our peace and spiritual and emotional sustenance, lies within the pages of this anthology."

~ Riham Adly, author of *Love is Make-Believe*

"I read this fascinating collection of 40 women's responses to the prompt *'Who Am I Today?'* in one sitting, not so much lingering on the many nuggets of raw insight or revelation, though they are worth lingering on—rather, allowing the voices to wash over and through me. Voices of mothers, daughters, widows, wives, victims, survivors, all seemingly striving to feel seen, heard, believed, known, celebrated. The cumulative effect was powerful. Jen Minotti's beautifully conceived anthology will resonate with women of all ages and identities. Bravo!"

~ Deborah Sosin, author of *Charlotte and the Quiet Place*
and *Breaking Free of Addiction*

"The heartfelt stories and poems in this inspiring, wide-ranging anthology will resonate with women from many walks of life, paying testament to the truth that the more we share what's in our hearts, the stronger we become, individually and together. This is a collection to savor, to return to, and to share."

~ Jennifer Browdy, PhD, author of *Purposeful Memoir
as a Quest for a Thriving Future*

"'Everyone is an equal access point within the circle,' states facilitator and author, Jennifer Minotti in the introduction to the Women's Writing Circle Anthology: *Who Am I Today?*, a beautiful collection that sprung from her years of gathering women in a safe circle of truth. Each circle Jen facilitates begins with the simple question: *'Who Am I today?'* This check-in inquiry allows each woman to take an internal snapshot of herself as an entry into what is coming up for her. This collection of essays, poetry, and prose showcases the words of 40 women who have answered that question with honesty and courage.

Touching on such intimate topics as fear, identity, hope, aging, grief, and faith, these remarkable women remind us that the circumstances of life are ever-changing, shaping and defining us in powerful ways, and that by writing and sharing our truth we are not alone on the journey."

~ Lisa Lucca, author of *Ashes to Ink: A Memoir* and radio host of *Live True*

"Writings in this emphatic collection portray the real lives and beliefs of and by women, resoundingly declaring, without any apology or guilt, who they are, who they were and who they wish to become. This is an endearing collection of poems, flash non-fiction and memoir with universal appeal on the theme of *Who Am I Today?* The writings reveal the exultations, anticipations, fears, and tears of women delving into the contours of their identity, one which they garner themselves, or which others or circumstances might envelope them with. In the end, the women writers in this anthology give a clarion call to the tremendous love and belief they hold for themselves and their capacity to be whosoever they wish to be. A word of high appreciation for the editor, Jennifer A. Minotti for her tireless efforts in not only bringing out this volume, but also in encouraging women writers to express and find their voice!"

~ Anita Nahal, PhD, author of *What's Wrong with Us Kali Women*

"'Open the window wide, dear,' writes Raluca Buttner in this marvelous collection that will open your heart and just might make you believe, as Buttner does as she writes, that being just might be enough.

Writing, I've come to believe, is as basic a human activity as eating, breathing, and seeing—a sacred right and rite. How else are we to catch the moments that fill our fleeting days! How else are we to know who we were, are and can be! While the act of writing may not change our circumstances, it prevents us from being owned by them. By sharing writing in loving community, we gain courage and resilience; find wisdom, love and delight. This book is a gift and a miracle. Read it and read it—and write!"

~ Leslie Lawrence, author of *The Death of Fred Astaire: Essays from a Life Outside the Lines*

"*Who Am I Today?* is a stunning collection of poetry and prose. This small and important book touches on everything from aging, cancer diagnosis, motherhood, grandmothers, ethics, religion, wonder, hope and grace, and gratitude. These brilliant women write not just for themselves but for every woman. Don't miss this superb and mighty anthology."

~ Laura L. Engel, author of *You'll Forget This Ever Happened— Secrets, Shame, and Adoption in the 1960s*

For all women

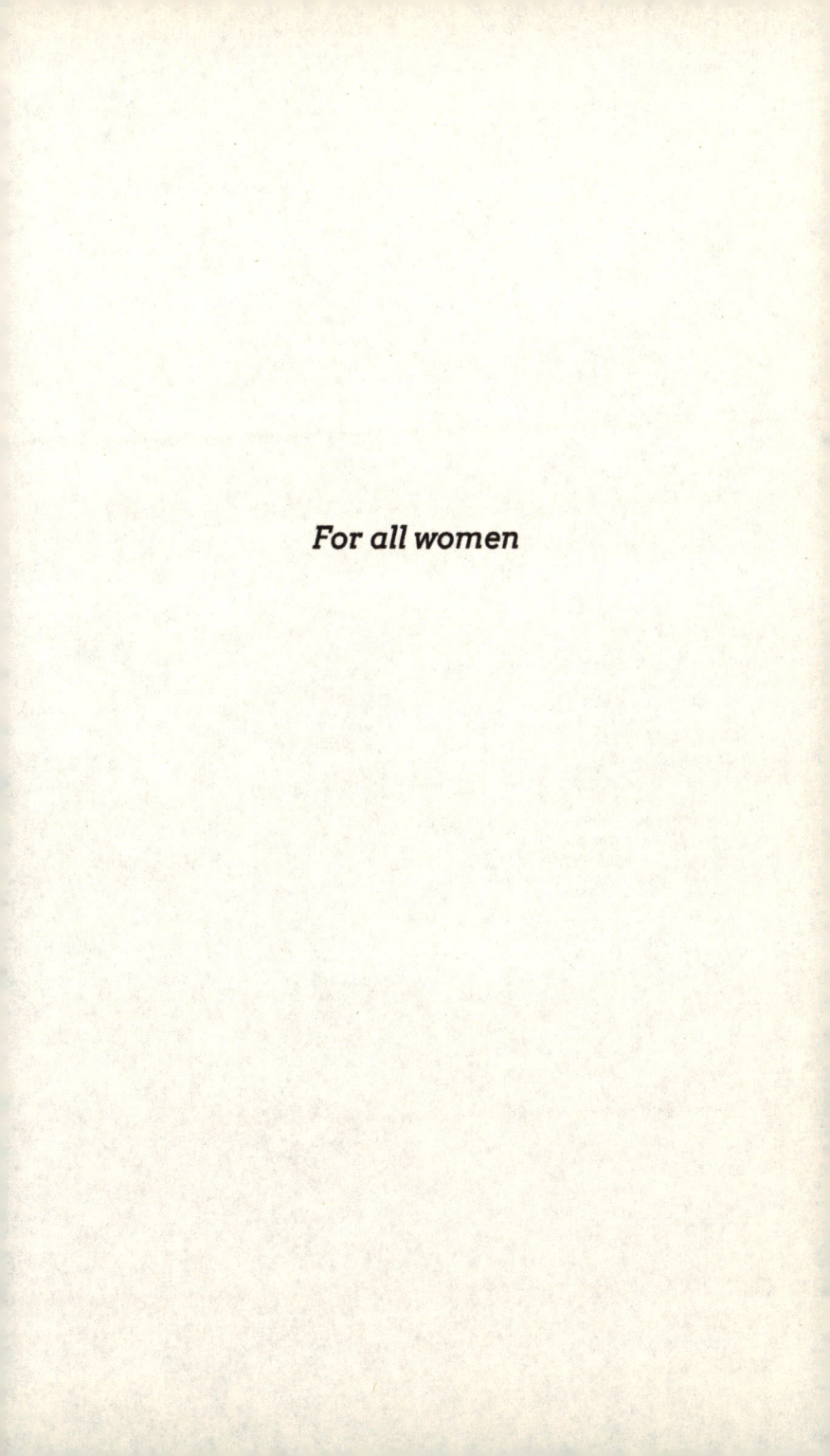

Who Am I Today?

An Anthology—
Voices from the
Women's Writing Circle

Edited by
Jennifer A. Minotti

Center for Women's Health & Human Rights
Suffolk University
Boston, Massachusetts

Copyright © 2022 by Jennifer A. Minotti

Women's Writing Circle
Center for Women's Health & Human Rights
Suffolk University
73 Tremont Street
Boston, MA 02108

Cover & Page Design: Jennifer A. Minotti

All rights reserved. No part of this book may be reproduced without written permission by the publisher, nor may any part of this book be reproduced, stored in a retrieval system, or transmitted in any form or by any means— electronic, mechanical, photocopying, recording, or other—without written permission from the publisher.

Printed in the United States of America

ISBN 979-8-21-173898-0

Who Am I Today?

CONTENTS

Introduction by Jennifer A. Minotti   1
Foreword by Amy Agigian   9

AUTHORS

Abha Das Sarma	13
Raluca Buttner	14
Barbara Simmons	15
Deirdre Maher	17
Christine "Cissy" White	20
Barrie Levine	27
Andrea Twombly	31
Cigeng Zhang	32
Donna Truong	33
Adeola Sheehy	35
Debra Dolan	38
Audrey Geliga	41
Lisa Friedlander	43
Amy Donahue	45
Jyotirmaya Thakur	47
Noelle Lee	48
Dipti B	51
Melanie Devoid	54
Jessie North	56

Terri Lee	59
Julie Johnson McVeigh	63
Amy Agigian	65
Paula Hagar	66
Jyoti Nair	69
Noelle Sterne	71
Joni B. Cole	75
Renu Sarah Thomas	77
Taslim Jaffer	79
Nancy Smiler Levinson	81
Jennifer A. Minotti	83
Kelly Easton	86
Sylvia Alberta	87
Crystal James	89
Courtney Glover	92
Donna Kmetz	93
Áine Greaney	95
Anjana Deshpande	97
Rose Loving	99
Sarah Birnbach	101
Marjorie Moorhead	104
Author Biographies	105
Acknowledgments	115
About the Editor	118

INTRODUCTION

By Jennifer A. Minotti, Editor

> "Having empathy for ourselves
> increases our capacity to listen to others."
>
> — Oren Sofer

Founded in 2014, the Women's Writing Circle (WWC) was created in order to provide a safe and nurturing place for discussing truths, sharing vulnerabilities, and bearing witness with compassion and gratitude to women's stories. As the founder and facilitator, I encourage women to embrace their authenticity and welcome whatever comes up in their writing without judgment, accepting all of it for what it is trying to teach them. But this isn't always an easy process. For many of the women who attend the WWC, this may be the first space where their voices and words aren't silenced, nor met with disputation. For this reason, I ask them to be compassionate with themselves.

Gathering in circle, women write from a series of prompts as an entry point to exploring emotions, personal histories, shared truths, joy, grief, and all of the things that matter most in their hearts. Sometimes my prompts are a word or a photograph. Other times they are a sentence starter. I often read poetry and compelling quotes. Sometimes I play music or have them smell something unknown. The specific instrument is not important. What is important is what these tools do to elicit and channel memories, thoughts and feelings. Intention is the point.

"We are in this circle to speak as honestly as possible," I tell participants, because sharing our truths is the pathway towards freedom. Some might argue that this is "navel gazing." I disagree. I believe deeply examining and speaking our truth is an act of courage that when extended outward, becomes a gift to the world.

Using expressive writing, positive psychology, and mindful communication strategies as gateways for transformation, women write for a specific amount of time without regard to form, structure, spelling, grammar, or punctuation. They then share their writing out loud, while the other participants remain silent in order to listen. As the facilitator, I encourage participants to be brave, vulnerable and sympathetic truth-seekers in both sharing and witnessing each other's personal stories. There is never any pressure for women to read their writing aloud if they don't feel comfortable, and I always tell participants that "passing" their turn to read is also a form of participation.

In addition, there is also no criterion for being a "writer" and anyone may join the circle. The WWC is open to all ages of participants who identify and/or express themselves as women; in fact, I have worked with women between the ages of 14 and 78. The only requirement for participation is that women show up as they are, prepared to use this space as a sacred time for themselves, and that they are generous in their hospitality and big-hearted in their service to the others in the circle. In this way, my hope is that women can experience being participants, as well as global organizers of empowerment, change and peace.

Often we don't know what we're thinking until we write it down. Over the many years that I have been facilitating the WWC, I have found that this type of no-pressure, expressive writing process supports both individual and group well being. This is one of the great benefits of expressive writing. As writers, we are continually trying to uncover the truth, unearth what's underneath the conscious. As women, we perseverate about the past, present and future—and everything that this necessitates—especially in times of turmoil. As human beings, we worry and care, scrutinize and explain, concern ourselves instinctively with the emotions of others. Ultimately, we organize and convene because we care.

People say that we create what we can't find. This is what happened for me. It was 2012, I was living in Vermont with my husband and two young children, and working full time. Joy was all around me, yet I felt suffocated by my environs. By day, I started to lose my voice, because when I spoke up, I was often met with judgment, rivalry and attitudes significantly different from my own. By night, I regularly woke up choking for air. Eventually, I started to pull away from those closest to me.

But I always found comfort in my journals, which had been steady, sympathetic companions since middle school. As I poured my emotions onto the pages, I always felt more balanced. At some point, as a researcher by profession, I wondered why this was. Back then, little was written about expressive writing in mainstream media, however, I soon discovered a growing body of research being conducted, most notably by visionaries James Pennebaker and Kathleen Adams. And then I had a thought. What if the positive emotions I experienced while journaling alone were even greater in a circle of kind-hearted, compassionate women? That's when the idea for the Women's Writing Circle was born.

People are often surprised when they hear me say, "I don't like groups," especially when they find themselves in one of the many groups I've started or joined over the years. But as a Jew (>0.002% of the world's population), 1st generation American (on my mother's side), INFJ (rarest Myers-Briggs personality type), Cancer (only zodiac sign ruled by the moon), and woman (social scientists actually study us as a subordinate group!), I don't really like groups for their hierarchies and homogenous nature. I often feel out of place or worse, pressured to conform or fall into line based on someone else's perception of my standing in the world.

However, I do love circles for their constant flow of inclusivity that has no boundaries. There are no beginnings or endings, which means no one was here first and no one was last. There are no institutional or historical power structures that disadvantage particular identities. No majority characteristic cultures that we have to adhere to in order to belong. No preconceived positionalities. No one is more or less privileged because they are part of a dominant norm. Everyone is an equal access point within the circle.

A circle is a place where supremacy cannot draw breath.

And where deep listening is the valued currency of hospitality.

The late global spiritual leader and activist Thich Nhat Hanh said that if we do not practice listening to ourselves, we will very quickly lose our ability to sit and listen to others. This is why it is still very important to write alone. But we also need spaces to practice being better listeners with others. "It takes two to speak the truth," Henry David Thoreau wrote. "One to speak and another to hear." This philosophy is at the heart of the Women's Writing Circle. Yes, we are able to write independently. But we gain power and strength when our voices are heard by others, especially as women. Research supports this.

The Women's Writing Circle offers a safe space to practice a kind of collective responsibility in holding and supporting other women's voices. Krista Tippet, the award-winning broadcaster, calls this type of activity "a generous act of hospitality" that is rarely done anymore. And that's because deep listening not only involves being attuned to what we are feeling, but also allowing others' words to penetrate our mind, body and soul. It involves being fully present, open, compassionate, and receptive. Deep listening involves a willingness to offer one's self as a witness, munificently receiving and absorbing the words of others.

For this reason, the WWC does not allow for verbal critique or dialogue. Just listening. I believe this enables women to fully trust themselves and their writing. Knowing that they can read and let go of whatever they are feeling—without feedback— brings about a level of comfort that is different than if they were to be critiqued in any way. Writing to be *heard*, simply put, is different from writing to be *assessed*. This is similar to any type of discussion. When there is intentionally no winning or comparing of each other's stories, someone writing about their morning coffee is as equally valued as someone writing about a traumatic event. And because women do not show up in order to convince each other of their viewpoint, they often emerge interpersonally and collectively more unified.

So why do I start each circle with the simple writing prompt: *"Who Am I Today?"*

"I do this intentionally," I tell women, "not because I'm lazy," and chuckle. I give this prompt repeatedly, because writing about who we are on any given day is a way to check in with ourselves, to see what is coming up for us, and to use the medium of writing as a way to introduce ourselves to the others in the circle. I also tell participants to save these 5-10 minute expressive writing pieces. Even though they may not seem like much, each time they write to this prompt, they are recording what's going on in that moment. Looking back days, months or years later, they will be able to see what they were feeling. More importantly, they will have a record of how far they have come.

Each and every time I give this prompt, I am blown away by what women produce in just a few minutes.

This anthology is extremely special to me, because on these pages, you will gain a glimpse into the thoughts and feelings of 40 women—including myself—who courageously wrote (for 5-10 minutes) to the question, *"Who Am I Today?"* When I sent out the call for submissions, I wrote, "If you have something to say, send it to me. If you're not sure if it's 'good enough,' 'finished enough,' 'enough enough,' send it to me anyway. If you're feeling sad, write. If you're feeling joyous, write. If you're feeling fed up with society, write. Trust me, I want to hear your voice. And so do others."

The writers in this anthology come from all backgrounds, numerous US states and countries (including India, England, China, Ireland, Canada, and Dubai), and (except for two women who signed up but were unable to attend) all have participated in a Women's Writing Circle facilitated by myself or Joni Cole in either Massachusetts, New Hampshire, Vermont, or via Zoom. Some works are titled. Others are not. Each response is special —some shorter, some longer—because each writer in this anthology is unique.

"People need people," my beloved grandmother used to tell me. I didn't fully understand what she meant until that time over 10 years ago when I felt myself needing other women the most. It was at that moment when I discovered the power of the circle. And all of you.

Thank you for hearing our voices!

FOREWORD

by Ann V. Angiolillo

In 2014, I was looking for a writing group on AboutUp and stumbled into a nearby Women's Writing Circle in Cambridge. Fill in few with the format—what people wrote, the facilitator Miranda—the whole thing. I begged Jen to bring the Women's Writing Circle to the Cigar Bar Women's Health and Human Rights at Suffolk University, where it fits so well into our mission and vision. Luckily, for all of us, she agreed, but e 2015 she has been holding regular Women's Writing Circles at the Center, where she is Writer-in-Residence.

There is something magical that happens in the WWCircles which is hard to put one's finger on. It's a combination of templates and intuition. Jen is a highly skilled and gifted facilitator, who sets the tone of each circle with her own energy, structures, and meditations. Women reflect, listen, and then write for short bursts in response to the prompts that Jen crafts. (Compulsory, but the first is always "Who am I Today?" This anthology grew from some of the prompts of this prompt.)

After we write, we have the opportunity to share in the circle. If we choose to read our words, the only response the other writers give, if they wish, is "Thank you." The deep give

8

FOREWORD

by Amy Agigian

In 2014, I was looking for a writing group on MeetUp, and stumbled into an early Women's Writing Circle in Cambridge. I fell in love with the format, what people wrote, the leader—Jennifer Minotti—the whole thing. I begged Jen to bring the Women's Writing Circle to the Center for Women's Health and Human Rights at Suffolk University, where it fits so well into our mission and vision. Luckily for all of us, she agreed. Since 2015 she has been holding regular Women's Writing Circles at the Center, where she is Writer-in-Residence.

There is something magical that happens in these circles, which is hard to put one's finger on. It's a combination of tangibles and intangibles. Jen is a highly skilled and gifted facilitator, who sets the tone of each circle with her own energy, structures, and meditations. Women reflect, listen, and then write for short bursts in response to the prompts that Jen crafts. Prompts vary, but the first is always *"Who Am I Today?"* (This anthology grew from some of the fruits of this prompt.)

After we write, we have the opportunity to share in the circle. If we choose to read our words, the only response the other writers give, if they wish, is "thank you." The deceptive simplicity of the process elicits deep listening and vulnerability. To track the impact of the Circles, Jen asks each participant to write three words at the beginning of the Circle, describing how we feel. At the end of the Circle, we again each write three words. Jen then reads aloud the before and after words, and we can see how the group as a whole has gone from words like stressed, exhausted, worried, sad, and lonely to words like joyous, relaxed, connected, peaceful, and grateful.

I wanted to bring the Women's Writing Circle to the Center for Women's Health and Human Rights at Suffolk because it fits in perfectly with our ethos: a humanistic vision of bodily integrity, gender equality, and social justice. Especially in this time of attacks against women's sovereignty over our bodies and our lives, it's so important to get women's authentic voices out there. Women's lives, knowledge, and words matter.

The Women's Writing Circle is important for both process and product. The process of expressive writing is powerful, and powerfully feminist. The courage it takes to face, share, and hear our diverse truths is liberating. Finding one's voice and being respectfully heard and validated is such a key aspect of shaking off the patriarchal conditioning to minimize our own knowledge and "go along to get along." At the same time, the "product"—the words you are about to read—is equally important. What is the truth about our lives in this moment?

I always look forward to the Women's Writing Circles, which are high points punctuating my year. I find that no matter how I'm feeling when I start—how busy, how impossible it feels to carve out the time—afterwards I feel much better: connected to the other women in the Circle and reconnected to myself in a nourishing way. I wish everyone could come.

In a recent Women's Writing Circle, I put onto the page what I absorbed from that same Circle.

> *It may not have been much, but I did this: today I learned that we are lonely, sick, in pain. We are worried, wanting to help those we love. We are tormented by violent men, unhelped. We live where we can see trees and birds and changing leaves. We have kids and divorces. We listen to poetry. Today I listen to everyone. I'm so glad the ant was saved with its unfathomable heart. Today, I learned, we have regrets, disappointments. We have love, loss. We are swimmers, writers. We are growing, changing, alive, hollowed out, wise. Today it may not have been much, but I showed up, slowed down, and wrote a few words.*

I hope that you will feel some of the strength and beauty of the Women's Writing Circle when you read this anthology. And I hope it will encourage you to speak your truth and stand up for your life and the lives of those others who are rarely heard but have so much to say. May you find an audience of deep, caring listeners who believe you and want you to thrive. And maybe even pick up a pen yourself.

Who are you today?

Abha Das Sarma

AS IT ALL FADES

Half buried in the past and no takers for what it was
Unwilling to let go of creations from years ago,
As the afternoon sighs and takes a deep breath
Why am I adding to this already burdened world,
Adding my sorrows, adding my cries
Adding little joys and more words, instead
Let me listen and watch
The falling leaves as the breeze goes past,
Walk the uncertain still stumble over things
Gently forget the gray and the unfinished,
Let me slowly slide
Out of the frame of this life.

Raluca Buttner

WHO AM I TODAY?

Feeling old
and with nothing to show
for these many years.

Open the windows wide, dear,
the moths are flying again
fluttering their fearful papery wings
too late, too late, too late
Is it too late to begin?
The mattress so brittle,
full of years wasted...

On a pacing day such as this,
echoing with "I wish"
I saw the trees,
still, standing,
empty handed without apology,
and thought perhaps,
perhaps,
being just might be enough.

Barbara Simmons

WHO AM I TODAY?

I'm someone who's worried about the flashing light I've begun to see out of the corner of my left eye, worried enough to have looked it up online in one of those medical sites where conditions can be investigated with the privacy of one's computer queries, but where the concerns linger long after the computer screen has dimmed. And, given the possibilities that I may have more than floaters, and, in my aging, might need to see someone for retinal care, I am always looking around, literally, to see if I can catch a glimpse of that itinerant flashing light, hoping to capture the invader to my vision and lock it away, at least for a while. It makes me think of all that I have on my bucket list to SEE, how important vision is to me to be the traveler, the reader, the viewer, with eyes appreciating the scene, the foods, the colors, the cadences, the rhythms, the words, the pages, the screens of all the visuals that have kept me longing for dawn after every dusk. It's made me remember the kinds of light that have informed my world: the rooms that are lit so softly that all within is contained without edges; the paths that are laser-beamed by flashlight that have led me to discover there's always more beyond the darkness; the pinpricks of a starry night that reveal so many bodies of light so much older than I, so much farther away than I'll ever travel, that all I can utter is thank you. Something I read a year ago, when the lockdown from COVID began, said that just as we're gradually losing our hair...and our athletic prowess, we gradually are gaining emotional stability and life satisfaction. I may not have all of my sight, but, I think I know that my vision is better than it's ever been, and my horizons can only be described as infinite. Who am I today? Someone who will still have REMs, will still dream, will still imagine a world, even if my eyes cannot see everything clearly.

Deirdre Maher

WHO AM I TODAY?

I am the old woman with stiff knees
I am the little girl with long, long hair
it falls all the way down my back
I am the woman giving birth
ankles bound in leather straps
legs held apart
I am a hundred waking nights
with a crying baby
I am the small child clutching
Twinkle magazine
eating an HB brunch ice cream
on the seafront in Salthill
I am the Irish immigrant mother
waiting at the school gate
in a leafy London suburb
I am the woman you see
alone in the supermarket
with tears behind her eyes
I am the widow
Once a wife
There are millions like me
And I am unique.

After you died, I thought I would have time to do many things, but I found I did not wish to do those things without you. I want to be loved but you knew me to my core and who will love me now? Thirty-one years ago I wrote this to you:

> "Now is my heart's desire fulfilled.
> All I most wished for has been granted to me,
> because you are in love with me."

There was never a place for me in the world until I found myself in your arms. Always on the outside, the third child, the third in a world of two by two. Accepted but excluded. A strange and solemn child; a plain girl filled with longing; an ordinary woman; an immigrant, no longer of the old country, not truly accepted in the new. None of it mattered when we were together.

Now I must make my way without you. How do I find myself? How do I negotiate this sea of grief? The waves rise to engulf me. I emerge gasping, blinking in the wintry warmth of the sun on my face. A million sparkles surround me on the surface of the water. I search for you in every one.

A therapist once asked me to write my name in the center of a blank sheet of paper. Like this:

Deirdre.

You are Deirdre, she said but you have many roles. I traced lines outwards like sunbeams from my name. At each end point I wrote one word. Wife, Carer, Mother, Daughter, Sister, Aunt, Colleague, Friend. Facets of a diamond? That's what you called me, your diamond.

I am some of those things still, but not all. "Whatever's remembered, lives." You are never far from me.

I will rise above the waters carrying my love with me. I will float on new wings. I will invite abundance and welcome joy. I will look to the future without flinching. I am alone but I can be happy alone. This is what I tell myself.

> So who am I today?

I am Deirdre. I am a writer. I am a poet. I am me.

Christine "Cissy" White

WHO AM I TODAY?

"I'm tired of fighting," I tell my palliative care contact, Jen via Zoom.

"It's not a fair fight anyhow," she said, "and exhausting."

It's not just ovarian cancer I'm tired of fighting though. It's the "fuck cancer" framework that's simplistic and insulting as well as the denial of others I'm done with.

I can no longer listen to how healthy I look, how long I'll live, or how fine I'll be. These words never make me feel better. I've had surgery, 11 cycles of chemo, been in a clinical trial, and my oncologist says the cancer is growing and the treatment options are shrinking.

It is not pessimism to reckon with reality. I refuse to waste time at war with what is, even when it's not the reality I'd have hand-picked. I don't want to fight about what's true in my life.

Denial and anger may be shields to hide behind and more familiar than sorrow but neither is worthy of my time.

Maybe I should say to my partner:

"Thank you for loving me."
"I'm sorry my disease is hard for you."

"Planning for death is difficult."

I want words to be bridges instead of weapons, want them to offer solace and protection like bandages do for well-tended wounds. Instead, our words are rubbing each other raw, leaving open cuts dirty, oozing, and on the verge of infection.

How can I say, "I want you holding my hand when I'm dying but I'm afraid my death will kill you."

How can I say, "If I can't save my own life shouldn't I at least try to save yours?" Your heart is bound so tightly, fear it will stop beating or explode. How can I say, "I know you love me but you clearly aren't capable of coping right now."

It feels like we're in a car on the highway. I'm in the passenger seat. You're driving. The hood flies up and opens blocking the windshield and our vision. I say slow down. Pull over. But you keep pretending we aren't in any danger, won't run anything over, that this ride is like any other. You shush me, insist I'm being alarmist, and negative.

You say you are a cup half-full sort of human but don't notice how you use your water to drown me out.

It feels like you are always pointing at the horizon making sure I look ahead as though I'm not consumed already and staring at the water as I vomit over the railing.

Don't you think I want to be the woman in the colorful dress, with the sunglasses and the relaxed look on her face, who smiles and holds the hand of her child who squeals in delight? They are new and bright and full of promise, their sky and future spread out wide while I am picking through the past, stumbling to the storage room below deck searching for a life vest so I can tread water a bit longer.

Still, even from where I stand, there are sacred seconds and stories I want to share. Still, what I am experiencing is holy and sacred.

Sometimes I'm a shell floating in the sea letting the water hold and buoy me. Sometimes I hold her water in the cup of space that is my center and become a boat, a home, and house the adventure of something even smaller. I'm tiny, but still important, useful, and beautiful. As a seashell I learn how to turn over, empty out and rest. I let the sun boil off the chill till I am dry. I hover, ebb, and flow by the tideline, learning to accept being in or on land, being tossed upon or taken underwater.

I'm so alive and still transforming.

I take in the smell of cinnamon held close to my nose or sprinkled over my coffee. I take in the smell of the damp dog as I rub her down after our walks. She likes to lean into me knowing it's time for her towel message. She lets me rub her wet belly and muddy feet.

I take in the smell of vanilla lotion as I rub my hands together, slightly sticky and warm, grateful for all the ways age lets us learn to mother our own skin, taste buds, and passions.

The leaves crinkle underfoot as I go to get the hanging ferns. They are no longer lush, lively, or sun-kissed but still, they are still alive. They are ready to be moved in for the winter, bundled up and rehomed until it's safe to go outside again.

I bite delight and let sensations sting me back repeatedly. I call it joy stalking and it's a daily practice that keeps me from dwelling in doom.

The lavender plant in my driveway still has bits of purple. I bend down and touch, rubbing the scent into my fingertips, and stop to appreciate the aroma, grateful for my effort to plant and tend, and its willingness to open and bloom in return.

When my daughter would get stressed about tests, I'd invite her to smell the lavender or notice the pink, blue, and purple shades of the hydrangea, her favorite plant.

Now she is a young woman who sends me photos of the hot cider she sips with friends at a cafe I've never been to today. Without any words, I am transported and feel her joy. Another day she sent me a photo of the coffee she is drinking on her way to class.

"What's on top?" I ask. "Is it cocoa or cinnamon?"

"Cinnamon," she says, and even without it near, I take it in, take her in, away from home, but as close as the scent on the tip of my nose.

I won't stop living.
I won't stop loving.

I get to be the woman at Petco looking for kitty litter. I get to be the mom texting and calling my daughter. When she says, "My classes are so terrible. I have two classes, two labs at 8a.m. at 8 am." she repeats as though it's a swear or tragedy.

I am not the mom who says, "You're lucky to be alive" or "cha-ching cha-ching cha-ching" who silences her by reminding her how much those horrible courses cost. I meet her in this moment, and say, "I'm sorry you didn't get the classes, professors, or times you wanted because I know how hard you work and how carefully you try to curate your schedule."

I may not make it to 60 but I can make green bean casserole and crisp today, knowing my lover will not be eating with us but at the table or at his tiny house in Canada where he feels close to his soul. There, he can record the pheasant, stand still under the dead and dark sky of night and find comfort among the countless stars overhead.

Hopefully, he will hear them call out to him brightly. They will calm, center, and steady his own beating heart as he learns to swim towards a future without me.

I whisper my final prayer as I let you go.

> *Think of me as the blueberry picked from the path you hand-cleared. Feel me near when you sit in the chair by your office and stare at the sky. Let me be the morning sun you stretch and wake into, warming you, reminding you how beloved you are. Let me be the steadiness in your step after you stretch out the aches, and try to start again. Know I'll always hover over and around you from boundless time, another country or galaxy away. I was grateful for your love, loyalty, and sharing frequent moments of sublime bliss. I will be as close as skin, as constant as heartbeats, and as invisible as the air you need to breathe. I will swirl*

and mix like the cream in your coffee becoming what you sip and ingest. Your rage will be forgiven, and in that melting where love is safe to return, maybe your rigid, hard edges will transform.

But today, I choose life, peace, and self-love because I'm still here and refuse to disappear myself for anyone.

I am the color yellow, relaxed, warm, a bit faded. I am lighter than butter, not as shiny as the sun, but my petals spread wide and outwards like a daisy.

I am the color gray, cloudy and deep, like a storm coming or the fog rolling in. I am hazy and thick and hard to see through even when I feel I've been transparent.

I am the red of rage, the red of blood, capturing all that is bright, raw, and vibrant.

I am no longer as fresh as the color green. I'm not new, young, and growing anything other than cancer and hope.

But oh how I have learned to appreciate the shades of brown, the crinkly, brown, damp, and decaying leaves at my feet when I walk - splattered with fading shades of what they were as they head for the next world.

Barrie Levine

WHO AM I TODAY?

I'm at a rest stop on the Mass Pike on the way home from a family event in Connecticut. I look over the parked trucks – some small and banged up, others so huge and decked out that my heart skips a beat – but I am one of them nevertheless, a member of the truck community with my own pickup.

The big black truck sat in the garage for six months after my husband Paul died in hospice on a dreary morning in December 2013. In the spring, I stepped up into the driver's seat and turned the key in the ignition. The engine fired reliably, then hummed sweetly. This is a sexy machine, a 2004 Tundra off-road model, black and shiny as Darth Vader's helmet. The graceful swelling over the wheel wells gives it the vintage look of an old farm pickup. But the best feature by far is that fearsome V8 engine.

This baby was a workhorse. We filled it with a yard of compost or mulch at the garden center. We bought a new washing machine and dryer and loaded them on the spot. If we found furniture at a yard sale, or a discarded playhouse marked "free" in a driveway, it came home with us. When we picked up our son and his family at the airport, we stacked their seven or eight suitcases in the bed, no problem. If a friend needed help with a move, we didn't mind at all. This gave Paul a chance to put his muscular vehicle to work. If a guy can love a machine, he was smitten with this one.

Sadly, he was stricken with an illness that, among its many cruel impairments, destroyed his ability to perform the simplest of tasks in proper sequence. I took away his keys when he began to operate the truck erratically. This is my most painful memory and a vision that haunts me still, how he sat in the truck, struggling to start it, at the same time not knowing why he was there or where he wanted to go. He flailed randomly at the handles, the steering wheel, the shift, the visor, telling me the truck was broken and begging for my help. If the tears I shed could fall on this page, these lines would be unreadable.

After his death, I assumed full title and drivership. The winter was harsh in every possible way, but I felt safe sitting high up on the road, looking over the black steel of the hood, supported by large tires and a dependable four-wheel-drive assembly. I looked out the windshield to the road ahead as my husband saw it. I felt the powerful engine as he felt it - and understood why he loved it in here.

Friends condemned the poor fuel efficiency – 14 mpg at

best whether city or highway – and urged me to trade it in for that reason alone. But I was coming from a different place, not about my level of eco-citizenship, but the need for day-to-day emotional survival. Navigating around jolting shocks of grief during my first year as a widow devastated me. Seeing the familiar black truck in the driveway each morning kept me sane. I stepped up into the cab and grabbed the wheel for dear life, seeking a cocoon, a safe place to remember – and to heal.

After the year like no other, the truck and I became inseparable. I brought home a dozen plants and shrubs that would never fit into the back seat of any car. I cleaned out our ranch house basement and carted truckloads of donations to a local charity. I moved my office equipment to the house without needing to rent a U-Haul. I powered out of snow banks or pulled out of a muddy ditch without a tow. I loved what the Tundra could do for me in all seasons, this Jersey girl who grew up on a suburban quarter-acre with no garage.

I look both ways, then turn onto the open road – and towards the future. I'm into my seventies now, moving along on roads I've never traveled, at speeds I hadn't reached before. You may see a black pickup with scratches and dents here and there, but formidable in its ominous appearance nevertheless, back up to the loading dock at the home improvement store. You watch the drivers' door open, expecting a 29-year-old contractor with tattoos on his arms to exit. Instead, out steps this 70-something woman with jeans, work gloves, and long silver hair. She slams the door shut and walks around to the tailgate, pulls it down with a metallic thud, then informs the guys that she's here to pick up her pallet of 200 patio bricks.

You'd say to yourself, this woman not only owns this truck, she owns her life - and you'd be right.

Andrea Twombly

WHO AM I TODAY?

Alone with coffee and my happy light piercing the early-morning cobwebs, I don't really know who I am today. Until you asked, I had the idea that I am simply a sixty-something woman, awake and wondering at the chipmunk feasting at the bird feeder outside my living room window.

And somehow, I had spent a few moments being my Essence. Pure Being. No comparisons, no regrets, no heartache.

But, since you asked, right now I am a sixteen-month-old widow, and since you asked, tears are rolling down my face once again.

I sit in silence. No morning news on the radio. Some break the silence with chatter and noise, but I prefer to bathe in it, listening.

Listening for any whispers that might sound from beyond the veil.

Cigeng Zhang

I AM A CORNER OF THE STARRY NIGHT

I stood on the bridge
Looking at the moon reflected in the river
Stars danced at the ripples
Wave after wave

A shoal of fish shuttled by
I heard the breath under the water
I saw twinkling scales
Shiny like little marigolds

I felt inferior to the fish
Fish could dive into stars and turn to flower
And I, just a dull shadow, staying
in the dark that was passing thru me

I lifted up my head to the starry sky
At a loss of thought
I took a deep breath like fish
Thinking, luckily I had eyes as inky as night

A poet I adored once composed it
Night gave me a pair of black eyes
I use them to seek light
True, I had the way to touch light even in darkness

Donna Truong

WHO AM I TODAY?

I've thought about this question a lot. For, like, my whole life, really. I've always struggled with my identity. I've asked other people who they are — what defines them as them, you know, to get some ideas, but it seems as though nobody really knows.

Growing up, I was always someone who just did what they were told and never really thought for myself. It was like, "Go to school, get good grades, and be polite."

Okay, yeah, cool until I actually needed to make my first real decision. "What was I going to major in? What will my career be?" I had one of many full-blown identity crises.

Not to mention, I was going through a breakup with someone who I was totally in love with and transformed myself into a person who I thought he would want. That's the problem when you don't know who you are. You don't hold your ground and you just change into someone you think you should be.

Though after I got over the breakup, I definitely found some confidence, because I was able to mend my broken heart. I still didn't know who I was or what I wanted. But I was able to distract myself with going through the motions of college, majoring in something that I thought would help me get a job, getting into a relationship where I again changed into a person who I thought my boyfriend would want because, really, my subconscious was telling me, "You …Whatever you are … You're not good enough. You have to be someone else." And, you know, going through social anxiety, because of the exact same reason.

It wasn't until recently that I challenged these thoughts. And, it all started with a book *The Power of Now*, where I had this revelation —

I am everything and I am nothing. I can be who I want at any given moment. Identity is an illusion, but I choose to be someone who is kind, open-minded, curious. and respectful. I choose to believe I am good enough and I am worthy. And, I do whatever I want because I am fucking free of other peoples' opinions.

Adeola Sheehy

THE LAKE

I look in the mirror and the reflection changes once more, it's as though I'm watching the surface of a lake as the wind travels by. There are brief moments of stillness where the image is identifiable, and then motion once more.

When I was a child I would be caught unawares by the sudden intrusion of the stranger on the surface as I walked by. Always surprised by that girl's eyes staring back at me surrounded by her frizzy hair and tanned skin. No matter how many times she appeared, I was always startled. Where was the princess, the girl I imagined myself to be? The words of Maya Angelou ringing in my ears as I moved faster, wanting to leave her behind.

"What are you looking at me for? I didn't come to stay."

Now when I catch that unexpected reflection, there are still often moments of shock. The gray that decorates my halo, the crinkles on my cheeks when I smile, the roundness that I'm not yet used to. In her eyes, I see the younger part of me, mischievous one moment and defiant the next, but she is held within the passing of the years, she has been tempered by my experiences.

This face responds to so many names now and seems to mold itself to fit the voices who call. The soft sigh of impatience to the child's demands, the smile that meets my partner's lips, the frown of concentration as I listen to the troubles of a friend.

All these subtle differences move across the surface.

The writer, the daughter, the partner, the friend who always has a shoulder and if you ask for it, advice. They all feel like parts, fragments of a whole that is being pulled apart to satisfy so many. Where am I and who I am under all the different hats I wear?

Under the surface of the lake that is always in motion.

I so often feel like there isn't enough of me, that like an elastic band if I am stretched any further I will snap, falling to the floor, no longer of use to anyone.

But in the moments where the wind briefly stops, and I see myself, I know that in truth, I am all of them.

They are all the one and the same to me. The water held in a lake doesn't change. There may be fluctuations in temperature, the sloping banks may erode a little with time, but the essence is the same. The weather that plays out over it and around it will cause its reactions. There will be calm days where the water's surface is still and reflective, icy months where at first glance the water may seem to have completely frozen over, and there will be storms that turn what was once inviting into a dangerous and foreboding place.

All these things only affect the surface, just as the changes on the surface of me, mean little to who I am.

I am a woman who holds space. I step aside within myself, so I can hear clearly the needs of my children when they call. Just as clearly as I can hear the words and their insistence to be written. The different needs of each individual are met with the corresponding reflection of me, but it is always me that greets them, hands open wide.

A welcome I can only give because the depths of me are mine alone, and that is where I lie, certain of who I am.

Debra Dolan

IN MY OWN TIME ...

TRIGGER WARNING

I am a woman who has forgiven my mother for marrying my rapist. It took me over 40 years, yet it has happened. Still feels so repulsive when I see the words strung together; another aspect of my lived experience to overcome. My mother was never without decency or kindness. She was a young mother. Over the years she has done a lot of nice things for me and I am grateful for so much. For most of my life I was profoundly conflicted about our relationship. In the 1970s my friends would comment that she was unlike the other mothers. She was sophisticated, well-groomed and sexy. Hannah's German accent was exotic and she dressed to emphasize her legs.

I did not understand what was happening between Keith and me when I was young. I was embarrassed to try to explain to anyone at first because I wasn't sure what it was. I remember thinking, "Wait a minute, was that right?" Looking back, I thought the kissing, fondling, and genital exposure was because I was special and I had a father's affection. I don't recall Keith saying that we had secrets, but I was aware it only happened in private. It was extremely confusing because I also loved him. One night he came into my room. He had been drinking and was breathing erratically. To this day I cannot stand the smell of beer on a man's breath. I instinctively knew that this experience with him would be different from the other times. I pretended I was asleep. I was wearing violet coloured baby-doll pajamas and he pulled them down past my knees. Then, he penetrated me deeply with his fingers. It hurt very much. I recall a sensation of disassociation, of separating myself from what was happening in that traumatic moment, of being the bystander to, rather than the subject of, this attack.

The next morning my rage burst. I told my mother what happened. I had pushed my dresser against the door so no-one could enter. I was crying. My mother was very upset. At a later point—it might have been a few days or a week—she told me that she had spoken to Keith and that what had happened would never happen again. And it did not. But the damage had already been done; the trust broken beyond repair. I became frightened of him. I did not want to be left alone with him. I bribed younger siblings, Christine and David, with my babysitting money to stay home with me while mom was at work, and when they would not, I attacked them. As soon as I was old enough, I left, and have not been back in decades.

Keith had been in my life since I was six years of age. My

birth father abandoned my mother and us children three years previous. Mom married Keith when I was a teenager. She married him in a civil ceremony at the courthouse months before she birthed a son; his first after three daughters.

It was not until my thirties that I understood that what Keith had done was rape, and that he had groomed me over time to gain my trust. A wrong had been committed against me, and no one stepped up to take responsibility. In addition to telling my mother, I told an older stepsibling and a teacher. No one responded with meaningful action. I was a child. The trust and security I relied upon in those most formative pre-pubescent years evaporated. I have worked very hard to regain them; alone and in my own way. I have learned that Keith died of natural causes in 2016 at the age of 92.

Audrey Geliga

WHO AM I TODAY?

I am someone who is confused but also at peace. I'm confused because as my children are getting older, they aren't as reliant on me as they were before and therefore, I'm not sure what to do with my life. For the last fifteen years, I've been "Warrior Mom and Advocate." And while I know that I will always be "that," the role isn't what it used to be. I thought I would dive full force into jump-starting my writing career. It's something that I've always loved to do. But as I researched and thought about it for a while, I struggled. I'm 46 years old. I don't want to have to stress about publishing a book, or how many followers I have on social media.

I left social media almost four years ago, and it's been a wise decision. So what do I now? I sought Reiki, meditation, and the advice of a few people I trust. As it turns out, I can do whatever I want! I've compared myself for years to my successful siblings, and that left me at times feeling unaccomplished and useless. Which is far from the truth. One of my siblings reminded me that if I hadn't stayed home and looked after my kids, they probably wouldn't have been as successful as they are now. I'm a Special Needs Mom and staying home was the best decision I've made for my children. This same sibling reminded me that I have lots of interests and I should try to utilize all them in the best way that I can. My life journey shouldn't be compared to anyone else's. Life is precious and I'm constantly made aware of that and reminded to try and live my happiest life.

And so, at first, I struggled and I was confused. Was I to become an insignificant being in this ever-changing, fast-moving world? No, you silly woman. You are so many beautiful things. You are the one who needs to slow down, and take it all in. Remember that you love to learn. You are constantly growing and the world is a plethora of wonderful things, waiting for you to explore and soak it all in.

This morning I am reminded by loved ones and the Universe that I am exactly where I need to be. While both of my children have had incredible progress throughout the years, I will always be a Special Needs Mom. I will always be needed for guidance, navigating, support, care, and maybe just a hug. Sure, I can pursue my interests and my passions. But I should never doubt for one minute that I am not important or useful. I will rid myself of those thoughts and remain the strong, loving, persistent Mommy that I am.

Lisa Friedlander

'I'-ING

Not 'I' the noun, a thing, an object, a word. No. Not I at all . . .

Leafing seems slow this spring up north in New Hampshire, the cold mornings dappled with sun and cloud but now, this morning, a swath of sun lights the crowns of the trees in our passing passing, passing by. Lightly scented rhododendrons flower into nose and lungs and I am not the flowers, but am nothing if not flowering. Foot-falling with the dirt path--that meeting of sole and soil that rolls and kneads with weight and wait and lunge does not describe my feet but rather kissing, friction, chuffing, thudding, toeing.

Ask about 'I'?

I: walking, straddling a large fallen log, seeing ducks ducking and diving on the thirsty channel to the lake, with the lake lake-ing, the sky sky-ing. Never enduring, never static, the 'I' neither a stopping point, a placeholder or a landmark.

I: unfindable, moving; not a belonging or list, even today.

So give a tight hug and make me 'me' for a moment. For a moment to you as a 'you.' Foster our mutual illusions of object permanence; of 'I'-ness and 'you'-ness; of lasting, fluttering love in the butterfly net of our arms.

Amy Donahue

WHO AM I TODAY?

I have started doing things. Things like sending an email to an old friend when I know I will be in her town. Like calling the men behind the gate at the natural gas facility over to me, so that I can explain how their security alarm is going off erroneously—waking me up in the middle of the night and in the early morning.

I am beginning to notice more—the large and small ways —I censor myself into inaction. And I am overriding that impulse, so that I might have some new things happen.

"My life is so boring!" I keep lamenting. But for anything new to take place, I am required to participate.

I see the simplicity of it in a way that wasn't accessible to me before. Maybe it's some critical mass of self-help books, therapy, and podcasts that all reach the same conclusions. After years of wondering how to construct the life I want, all sources seem to point back to the inevitable fact that I must do things. I must act. And that is not nearly as difficult as I have imagined it to be. By doing, I am becoming.

"I want to be a writer!" But I never sat down and wrote. Now I do, and I am. I didn't have to restructure my life, I just had to do things inside of it. It was so much closer than I expected.

Jyotirmaya Thakur

WHO AM I TODAY?

I am not a classic of super God's creation
Rather a parable of tears unseen
In the rhythms of my free verses of mighty sea
Formless as the clouds in the itinerary of the cacophony
My brown colour is shunned but not ignored by many
I abide within myself whose colours have worn away
I wish I could read my critics mind of hostility
As an immigrant of lost identity in translation
I am a poem of the heart that cannot be read openly
I am a stranger to readers with boundaries created
The cyclic curiosity goes on eternally
No one knows what it's like to be lost in the synthesis
Between dualism of humankind and monism of my maker
There is nothing as genuine as me although relatively deceptive
Maybe I am written as an ethical effect of modern artifact
Or just replicated from the lives of others who came here before me
I feel vague in my abyss of deep deep core
I came into this world as a drop of water
I accept no suppression and will evaporate soon
Yearning to create a vigorous ripple of freedom
In the majestic ocean and into the eternity of water.

Noelle Lee

WHO AM I TODAY?

At 32 years old, I seek to be sound in my values, statements and actions; to be the same on the inside and out. This is what's called integrity, the quality of being consistent in quality throughout; whole; undivided. I am a Christian through and through. Despite its increasing unpopularity in today's postmodern, post-Christian nation, I have made a lifelong commitment to live by the epistemic and ethical standards of orthodox Christianity simply because I have been called to believe; I just couldn't imagine any other path of life. Never mind that I wasn't raised Christian or did not come to the faith until I was 23, and that it took another 9 long years of learning and application to be ready to be baptized into my new church community.

I used to be a romantic libertine, in awe of classic punk bands and great art that examined what it meant to be and think about the world, the nation, the family. I believed Nietzsche's proclamation that "God [was] dead" and derived my theories of where knowledge came from from a hodgepodge of Western letters and derived my theories of moral behavior from Modern and later

Western literature, in which great romances, great human character and great moral choices were explored by way of human reason alone. Yet this was all possible because I had the privilege of safety, security, comfort, and art. Little did I know that this was all an immature and spoiled way of looking at the world and interacting with it.

Somewhere along the line, I began to see that there was an invisible network of order and meaning to life, and if not this, then the need for one. Perhaps it was witnessing the Recession of 2008 and the decline of America's economy and being jolted from the decadence and security of the 1990s to the scarcity and uncertainty of the late 2000s and 2010s. Suddenly, without the safety net of a secure economy, libertine values celebrating the individual who was free of the evils of religion seemed in excess and dangerously radical. There must be a God; for God to be dead, he must have existed at one point; isn't atheism simply a reaction to God, thus establishing that God or some form of God must exist? Religion may not be perfect, but it is a good start in that it gives a sturdy wall upon which to bounce off of. Without this wall, the bouncing becomes chaotic and meaningless.

Reflecting on my past secular humanism, I realized that it was only a function of economic security and privileges not had in most parts of the world, such as an intact biological family unit, quality housing and transportation, nutritious food, ample clothing to keep in sync with the season's fashions, and access to quality public education in the world's most developed country. Without these privileges, I would never have had the freedom and resources to explore beyond God and live a life of secular humanism. In a scarce and uncertain world, God becomes necessary to impose normative constraints on the darkness so that some order, some structure emerges. Without God, everything becomes possible, to quote Dostoevsky, and in the ceaseless, massless darkness of poverty and insecurity, such order and structure are necessary.

At 32, I have transitioned from a spoiled suburban teenager with ill-formed ideas on what life means to a young adult who has tilled her spirit to prepare to sow the seeds of the Christian life. I hope to reap much fruit by reflecting the God I believe onto the world, so that in this increasingly dark, formless and chaotic world, the faint outlines of order and the dignity of life can become clear.

Dipti B

I CONFESS, I WAS HAPPY WHEN THE ENTIRE WORLD WAS MOURNING

Year 2020. The very year of darkness. I don't think I need to talk much about how the year was like as we all have our own stories to tell. I too have my own story to share. I was a lost soul. Without having anybody to guide, I saw darkness everywhere. Then the world went dark. I was locked inside my own home, far away from outside world toxicities.

When the deaths rate started to surge, I got hit by a self-realization—What if I die? I was always invisible to everybody and felt like none would even care. I tried to think about all the good memories I had but I could not find much. There was nothing and nobody to truly remember. I realized I was just another lonely person in this planet.

Not many people know about this but it's not been long since I got diagnosed with hypothyroidism. Hypothyroidism is a condition where the thyroid gland cannot produce enough thyroid hormone because of which you will get certain symptoms varying from person to person. For that, one will be prescribed with certain medication like Thyronorm and you will be fine—yippee! But, it's not that simple actually. Well, at least it is not for me. What I used to experience was extreme fatigue, joint pain, drying of hair, loss of weight, and many more, but the most torturous one was feeling depressed all the time. It used to feel hard to even get up from the bed and do my basic chores. I used to feel like giving up. I used to feel like I was dying from inside. Every day felt like I was closer to death. I felt such all my life. I had those symptoms at a very young age but was always ignored. Nobody gave any attention to my changing habits, thinking I was just another annoyed teen. I did not give much attention to myself thinking I was just a useless brat.

After medication, I felt like a different person compared to my old self but somehow, that old me was still sticking around. I am not saying I am not okay now. I did (and I do) feel normal when I did not even know what 'Normal' felt like. For the first time in years! Yeah, after years of internal and physical battle, I am not scared of waking up in the morning. But after years of not having much human connection and fighting with myself, it affected me a lot. It feels like I lost my entire teenage-hood and some adulthood and I have regret for the things I could have experienced, other than just lying on my bed. I am somewhere in my 20s and I feel like I am just learning to crawl, when everyone is already running and reaching where they want to be.

That year, I further disconnected myself with several people with whom I could not even share my pain and journey. I also reconnected with some of my old friends. They did not complete my void, but I realized it's important to let some people in. That year, I danced every day, smiled almost every day even if I did not feel like smiling, took care of my "beauty," read some stupid romantic novels while criticizing its in-depth misogyny yet fantasizing a "prince charming," painted more than I imagined, and took lots of photographs with a smiling face. But above all, I created a small but significant memory of my own without anybody in the picture, and somewhere in between I realized I was healing—slowly.

Yes, 2020 became a good year for me despite having problems in our family and in the world, and despite losing people I knew. I have learned I cannot change the past and I cannot even change the grief I had, but I can learn to live with it, appreciate my journey, be proud of 'new' me, and be more open to this thing called LIFE!

Melanie Devoid

WHO AM I TODAY?

Wow! It amazes me to think about who I am today. I thought I knew but I don't, or do I? I'm just a seasoned woman who is going through a difficult period in her life again. I've been beaten down by circumstances that are beyond my control. I guess I'm a burned-out caregiver to my 94-year-old dad who is slowly dying of Parkinson's and dementia. I love my dad so much and am honored to spend this time with him. He is mild-mannered and is good to me in spite of his disease. It is a hard thing to watch and my tears of grief flow easily these days. I'm alone in this journey with him even though I have relatives that could help. Some do help now and again.

I do think about the fact that I don't do enough to take care of myself. I worry about that and know I need to do more for me. I have my excuses as to why I don't take care of me. I just always put everyone else first. You know, I am not worthy enough. I know not sound thinking. With my traumatic brain injury, I struggle to figure it all out. But this one thing I know for sure is that no matter how beaten down I get physically or emotionally, I will rise from the ashes of despair and live again. My experiences of abuse and difficulties in life have shown me the strength within me, my resiliency, and my ability to overcome the horrible things that life has thrown at me.

I am more than just a survivor of domestic and sexual violence. I am more than a survivor of a traumatic brain injury. I am more than someone going deaf. I am more than just a burned-out caregiver to my dad. I am me. I am a loving, kind daughter, mother, and grandmother. I was told after my car accident that left me with a traumatic brain injury, that I'd never teach again. Well, I am so proud that I've overcome that hurdle and I'm a college professor today and loving it. I still have my core knowledge from my many years of teaching and can now share with my students what I have learned. I am able to do that without any memories of being in the classroom. Snippets of my life will just come into my mind when I need them and often leave as quickly as they came. I may not have the memories, but I still have the knowledge.

It has, yet again, taken writing about myself to realize just who I am ... daughter, mother, grandmother, professor, volunteer librarian, friend, aunt, and yes, caregiver to my dad. I am all of those things in spite of exhaustion from doing too much. It's nice to be reminded as to who I really am.

Jessie North

WHO AM I TODAY?

I'm a woman with a past, developing her future
I'm a survivor, who wants more than just surviving
I'm middle-aged, but starting from the beginning
I'm educated, but have much to learn
I'm safe and secure, and scared shitless

I'm an adult child, raising her children
I'm shy, unless Mama Bear is needed
I'm a person, who happens to be female
I'm a role model, in need of a role model
I'm wise enough to know, I know nothing

I'm pulled backwards, but push forwards
I'm always falling down, but I always get up
I'm struggling to concentrate, and can't stop focusing
I'm connected to nature, and a slave to technology
I'm a member of society, and I keep to myself

I'm a traveler and philosopher, and a creature of habit
I'm a karma believer, I was blind and now see
I'm not afraid of the system, it already spit me out
I'm sad, but happy to make you happy

I'm a lover, and a fighter, and a peacemaker

I'm loud and extreme, and quiet and small
I'm full of doubt, and hopeful and optimistic
I'm a free-thinker, and a follower
I'm introverted, and extroverted
I'm strong, and I'm vulnerable

I'm a dancer, who feels as stiff as a board
I'm a reader, and a watcher, and a listener
I'm a teacher, and a student
I'm a consumer, and a minimalist
I'm alone, but not lonely

I am able, and disabled
I'm subtle, and flamboyant
I'm a dreamer, with nightmares
I'm raw, and well-trained
I've lived many lives, but still search for my own

I'm full of love, and anger
I'm a hugger, and a yeller
I'm fast, and I'm slow
I'm interested, and I'm bored
I'm free, and I'm chained

I'm a fan, and a critic
I'm poor, and I'm rich
I'm new, and I'm old

I'm human, and flawed
I'm a wimp, and a warrior

I'm a woman at the crossroads.
I'm old enough to know better.
I'm part of this universe.
I'm a wallflower with a voice.
I'm more powerful than I realize.

I'm a Writer.

Terri Lee

OPEN EYES

I am a 48 year old woman trapped in an 8 year old mind. Peering in the mirror looking at my eyes that don't open very wide.

I'm looking, pushing eyelids up and wondering if the fold will hold if I blink my eyes? How long can I go without blinking?

I'm the 14 year old searching the frames at the optometrist wondering if any will sit on my nose and clear my cheeks? Why, oh why did my vision go bad now?

I lived 48 years and this is the first year I allowed myself to remember. Remember how it REALLY felt to grow up Korean American in a mostly white suburb. I was one of the few Asians and one of the few non-Jewish families I knew.

I wished. And wondered how it might feel if I were at least Jewish? I could go to Hebrew school. I would be part of a community. I wouldn't be alone.

I was learning English amongst a community of Jewish families and no, I didn't know which words were Yiddish and which were English. I was struggling to fit in.

I was thrilled to be called a banana, a Twinkie! I mean, who wouldn't be thrilled to know that deep down you act, talk, and seem like every other white person around? I wasn't the type of immigrant wearing my shoes with the heels folded in like those other Asians. I was a bonafide American as long as you didn't SEE me.

I loved calling people.

But once you asked for my FULL name, reality struck and you learned that I am not white. I tried to hide—swapping my first name so it wasn't Korean and adapted my baptismal name as my first name. I convinced my parents when we were getting our citizenship to make it official. I am Theresa first. NOT Hery. I hoped that no one would ever ask me for my middle name. If they did—I left it at 'H.' That could be anything, right? Helen, Harriet, Hope. Let the guessing commence.

At 48, I'm feeling all the feels of suppressed reality and doing my best as a "passing" Asian American. I am hurt. Angry. Disappointed. Why did I humiliate other immigrant Asians including my own parents? Why did I feel proud to sound like an American? Why didn't I let myself feel when someone would tell me to go home.

Home? You mean to Rochester? I don't know any other place.

I came to America when I was 7 months old. And for 48 years I have been trying to understand who I am. Where I belong.

I spent decades assuming I couldn't be a writer because—well, my first language is not English, right? I can't speak Korean well, but because my parents speak English as a Second Language I, too must have poor English. I assumed I should never be in the public eye. Who would support an Asian actor, politician or musician? As an Asian—I am bound to become a mathematician, scientist or something very logical.

And yet—here I am 48 years later. A creator. Artist. Designer. I am spontaneous. A risk-taker. And I love all things that push boundaries. I have yet to follow the "normal" path of life.

I spent 48 years assuming I was just "one of those" weird ones. Failing at life over and over. I tried to remain as incognito as I could. Didn't seek fame, or a position of authority. I was a good cog in the machine of life. And while I kept spreading my wings and finding adventures, I would always return to accept something "normal" and try once again to ground myself in expectation and duty.

I have fought 48 years to hide my identity as Asian American.

But it's time. After 48 years, I am angry.

What is this society that tells me I don't belong? Who are you in the community whom continue to stay silent and let this be "normal?" Why did so many of us assimilate and just accept our place?

I am fired up. I am 48 years old and FINALLY realizing all that is bottled up inside. And it's time. It's time to Stand Up. It's time to demand change.

I'm ready to open up. Be vulnerable. Get fired up by the suppression of our society. It's time to come together for all my fellow Asian Americans.

Today my narrow eyes are open.

Julie Johnson McVeigh

WHO AM I TODAY?

I am a woman in change.
A woman birthing a new day, a new tomorrow.
A woman stepping into a new self, an old self,
my true self
to meet the day.

I am a woman who is curious, excited and trepidatious. I am a woman who is learning that I have feelings in a dust covered box that has laid buried under piles of tasks and successes
as I faced outward
forgetting to attend to my inward.

I am waking to find that I am still here
Waiting for me

to pay attention

to slow down

to find my cloak of courage

to step out naked into this world

to feel the cold against my bare breasts

and to know that I am alive.

I have another day
to live my truth
and to meet the world with it.

Amy Agigian

WHO AM I TODAY?

Today I'm not a pincushion and I'm not a blood bank. I'm not a dairy queen. I'm not the Many Breasted Artemis. Today I'm not here to make you smile. Who am I kidding? Today I'll leave you with a warm feeling whether I want to or not. Today I'm still itchy. Wanting so much. Greedy for myself and for the world—we can do so much better! Today I'm living in October. We still have seasons, though they're changing, getting harsher. Today I'm living in the generations, and none of us is getting any younger.

Paula Hagar

WHO AM I TODAY?

Last month I was a woman who spent 8 days alone, dying from fear and anxiety in the parched prickly desert near Tucson, not knowing at the time that I was plunging into a deep dark night of the soul. Today I am a woman reborn who has finally risen back into the light and is learning to fly with newly sprouted baby wings.

Darkness for me is too often all-encompassing—lightless, hopeless, helpless, body and mind pressed-down-flat-to-the-earth by negative thoughts and the giant shoe of life crushing me down. Even when there are days or weeks of no relief from the vast abyss, the one life vest I have always, always been able to see and grab onto is beauty, even though I forget about it in the dark. The sweet song of red-breasted house finches darting to and fro among the patio rafters, trying to settle on the perfect nesting corner; the scratch of the squirrel's claws on the screen door, begging and waiting patiently for a walnut, a cracker, an apple; the blue blue blue spring sky that exists only in Colorado, and comes and goes and shifts in minutes with equally mesmerizing white peony blooms of clouds. And right now—the peonies themselves that grow two inches a day, the magenta flash of blooming crab apples on every street, and the lilac buds getting ready to pop and bloom, as they always do, on my birthday in five days. It's harder to see the beauty of turning yet one year older again, especially after this past lost year, but I hold onto the relief that another year means I am still alive and kicking. I am not dying. I still have time and life ahead of me.

Today, and in these last stressful weeks, I've been thinking incessantly about hope. I'm not often sure just what it is, where it is, and how to grab onto it as the life preserver I need. But today, after weeks of depressing writing, I finally journaled my way out. I finally remembered that hope, among other things, lies in beauty, and my wonderful ability to always ALWAYS focus on it with every turn of my head. The tulips this year are the biggest and most bountiful they've ever been. Such tender beauty in the deep blackness of JavaJive, his golden eyes full of love for me, and for the same songbirds I love and feed—and his lazy basking beneath the bird feeders where he simply watches them, and never kills one—bursts my heart open. This old cat and the way his glossy blackness turns maroonish and chocolatey in the sun, and his sweet coos of joy melt my heart every time he sees me and every bird, moth, bug, dancing leaf. There is such wonder in his intense curiosity, even days later, at his first encounter with the scent of fresh sage bits I plucked at the Botanic Gardens on Sunday—another place full of nothing but brilliant flowers, earthy scents, ducks with fuzzy babies and that black-crowned night heron perched on a rock, waiting motionless to pluck a goldfish from the Japanese Garden pond—beauty in every glance, every breath.

All I have to do to reconnect with the world, to hold onto the light and hope that beauty in color, birds, all trees, art, sky, and LIFE can resuscitate me, is simply REMEMBER to just open my eyes and my heart. Writing can bring me back, but I forgot all this as I slowly swam through the darkness and back up toward the rays of light. Why do I keep forgetting this superpower of mine? Why do I have to keep remembering to remember to simply turn my head wherever I am and look and listen at any moment? There is beauty in every glance no matter where I am.

Today I am a woman who is remembering that beauty is my lifeline, and journaling helps get me back there when I forget.

Jyoti Nair

WHO AM I TODAY?

Who am I today?
Am I an audacious albatross?
Deliberately grimacing the sweat drizzling peony,
Who tries to kiss my scorched palms ...
My ribcage, a deserted shore, abraded by stinging yearnings?
During elliptical nights, my veins become fire-gargling albatrosses ...
Strangulating conflagration that guzzle twilight-tapestry,
Amethyst dew-breaths massaging my eyelids ...
Contemptible minutiae of my existence, that my windows swallow ...
Insouciantly ... With blasé breeze as forks!

*

And one day, presumptuously, I decide to choose the Aurora!

*

Aurora and I ...
If I am the tantalizing trapeze,
She (Aurora), the blithe gust dappling the cosmology ...

If I am the cataclysmic chimera,
She, the manacled magma,
The sensuous-sodden song,
Smoldering in my bones ...
Whenever I am tainted, she is flagellated,
While the world has been peering through her hues.
Her deepest hue, her vivacious veracity ...
She, the scourge, the wizened whiplash ...
Alas, they didn't care to fathom her seared silken skin ...
The world's psychedelic windshields, merely wish to
guzzle her as a balsamic ballerina.

Contrapuntal ...
Not an ethereal epigraph,
Aurora is the contrapuntal cuddle, between heavenly
harbingers ...
She is chiaroscuro, a tale that Southern Cross narrates to
Orion.
The crepuscule that dribbles from my dreams and dazes ...
Stitches my scattered nerve-fibers.
The feathers that flew-off from the Gouldian Finch ...
Perched on my barren palettes.
The chortling cherry blossoms that wrap my bare,
trembling shoulders ...
Cajole my palpitating deliriums.
The ostentatious oasis, that furtively craves to sneak into
charred desert quilt ...
Moistening my languished irises.

Noelle Sterne

IDENTITY

From my high-floor terrace, I watch the cars on the highway
scurrying forth and back,
Toys importantly skimming along.
I don't need to scurry or go—
Content to stay on my high floor here
All supplied—full refrigerator, enough clothes and appliances, crucial computer—
And write. That is who I am today
and every day.

Writer writer.

But, still to wrest meaning from life, constantly asking,
"Why life? What are we supposed to do, feel, aspire to, complete?"
Many answers, as many as self-appointed gurus lecture and blog—
Give love express create exchange experience feel reflect yield merge accept surrender
And know you can never get it done.

But no single answer satisfies.
The question echoes
From midnight to morning.
Except for a small while, despite work with clients, calls with friends, nods with neighbors,
for one answer.

Like now.
Sitting on my high-floor terrace
Clipboard in lap,
Glancing up from my notebook,
Surveying the highway and sky and trees,
Eyes and mind back down
To scribble again.

Time fills swells stretches enriches
Finally stops
And means something.

But for how long?

How long can my hand hold the pen?
How long can my wrists hang onto the keyboard, fingers flying?
How long can my mind stop the to-dos and surrender to Your words?
Not long at all.
But then, I reflect.
Hemingway published only seven novels, with three more

posthumously (but many short stories).
Mary Faulkner (who?) wrote 904 novels under six pen names.
Who's "better?" Certainly the lesser is the more famous.
Is quality the final arbiter? Is quantity?
Does it matter? What does it matter?

My cousin said, "I told my friends that when I die they should toss everything into a dumpster. None of it means anything except to me."
Is that how I feel, whatever my quality and quantity?
Yes, about everything—but the writing.
Three full books (one barely counts; it's for children) and many essays, stories, and poems in collections.
All the books sit proudly on my bookcase near the front door.
And in cabinets, files on files of all-stage pieces—some with intent to finish, some with notes hardly remembered. Others flat, aborted early from lack of interest.
But I can't get myself to throw them out.

Who would be interested in any of it?
A hunched-over ultra-earnest graduate student, laboring for an advanced degree for that coveted position teaching, a colossal lecture hall of freshman English at _____ University? Maybe, slightly.
A relative of mine? Hardly. They're tired of hearing about my infrequent successes in publications no one ever heard

of. And feigning congratulations.
Friends? In the middle of my reeling off a recent string, one cried, "Stop! Stop!"
Was she jealous? My productivity a reprimand to her retired state as artist, with her only creativity now ingeniously using leftovers?

No remedy. No final answer.
Except for one, today and every day the same, satisfying, unstoppable, yet shaky—

Who am I today?
Writer writer

Joni B. Cole

WHO AM I TODAY?

I've become one with my sweatpants. I'm way over-attached to this red, flannel shirt. My hair is a straw nest that hasn't seen a pair of sharp shears for over a year. Outside my pandemic bubble, the NEWS blares at me, "Let me in!" So many horrible horrors.

Inside my bubble—the space where I live and the space between my ears—the daily drama is not quite so urgent.

Drats, we're out of almond milk again.

Where did I leave that bobby pin; these bangs are driving me crazy.

Why isn't my audio working? Can you hear me now? How about now?

The pandemic has changed me. But not everything about me. Lip gloss! Always, the cheery familiarity of my red lip gloss. I love the way it soothes and shimmers. I love the way it pops on a Zoom screen. I love that word. Gloss. It sounds just like it feels.

Today, I tuck my lip gloss into the pocket of my skinny jeans. Ugh, already I miss my sweatpants. But the time has come to reemerge and that requires real pants. Who knew such a miracle was possible, that we would see an end, or at least the beginning of the end, of the pandemic by spring? And with it, a New Me, evolved during fifteen months behind a mask; fifteen months outside my previous everyday existence.

The New Me is less about hustle and more about naps. The New Me is more sensitive to suffering. The New Me thinks less about shoes and the color of her roots and more about grace and gratitude. Okay, sure, I gained a few pounds, but I also shed a few grudges. I let some things go. I'm (almost) done being mad at my stupid neighbor. And all it took was a pandemic.

I'm out the door. Man, these jeans are tight. It's spring! Breathe. Take it all in. World, meet Joni. Joni, meet World. Why do I feel so anxious? I pat my pocket; feel my trusty little tube of shimmer. This is my touchstone, my constant. If the New Me missteps, I won't beat myself up. Grace, I remind myself. We are all only human, surely that includes me. As long as I have lip gloss, it can all be smoothed over.

Renu Sarah Thomas

AWAKENING

She lay there flesh and bone, but was she really there?
Why did I come here? My soul to bare or again feel it tear?
Unseen, unwanted, I was that child no longer
Or was I? I reached out for food, but not for hunger.

O Child! Such pain the womb has caused you,
For the cord severed but just flesh and sinew.
The tongue pierced sharp to depths unseen
Why mother? Do you wish I'd never been?

Each turn I return here, to kindle a flame
A spark I look to fuel, but it feels just a game.
Banquets on the table are spread,
Tokens of love, then why feel I dread?

I hear my heart pump in the silence we share
See me mother! See that I care!
I re-awake your home, your mistakes I cover
I have become your nurse and yea, now your mother.

As I build you up, now others tear me down

Will life here never change? Will they forever frown?
A beast rises within me, I feel the heat redden my face
I growl, I roar. I will no longer be disgraced.

The curtain comes down on this little show
A battle won or lost I do not really know;
But a fight was fought, within and without
The chains have loosened and I know I must get out.

Freedom, pain joy and sorrow,
With all these will I still rise tomorrow
But new robes have I, and my shoes are tied,
I lift up my head, my destiny will not be denied.

In my joy I feel and now comprehend your pain
Of being unseen, living seemingly in vain
The heart must heal for the eyes to open
'tis only now I see you, for I am no longer broken.

Like you I am strong and live my life loud
We are who we are and of that I am proud
I know you loved me and that in me you saw you
This is the circle of life, where hope too is renewed.

Taslim Jaffer

WHO AM I TODAY?

I'm curled up on under a blanket on my metallic grey swivel chair, turned to look out the French doors that open onto the back deck.

To the side of the deck sit three cedar planters, filled with soil and promise; the gladioli shoots have pushed through thick and strong though I think it will be awhile until their brilliant flowers show. Lemony-yellow English violas, their petals outlined in light purple, dance a little in the breeze. Everything else rests under the dirt. Waits.

It's not a cold day but I am comforting myself in this in-between place of feeling unwell and ... better. This in-between place looks like fixating on the young green buds of the maple tree, breathing in the two-note call of the chickadees, peering at the house finches flitting from the feeder to the bare branches of the cottonwood tree.

My ears are roaring but muffled and I feel the way they sound—dull.

I notice the sunflower plants my friend gave me, there on

the edge of the deck. Five of them between two containers, and I see they have reached a little further toward the sky. Maybe they will be ready to transplant to the bigger planters this weekend. Maybe by this weekend, I will have reached a little further toward the sun as well.

Today, though, I am just an observer of everything growing around me. I don't know if I am like the dahlias below ground, dormant yet potential vibrancy, or more like the annuals on my front porch that rotted in the pots without proper drainage.

Today I am someone still living with a persistent dizziness, a fraction of who I think I would be if this didn't show up in my life and dampen my spirit.

But who am I to know who I might be then? I only know what is right in front of me, who I am, here in this chair.

A mom, a daughter, a wife, a sister.

A writer, a teacher, a student.

A soul.

I take in the scene of where I am today. It has fuzzy, unclear edges but also beauty—some of it I can't see yet.

It has potential and promise under a river of tears and darkness. I burrow deeper under my blanket.

Nancy Smiler Levinson

RISING

I first waved my wings as an angel
lying in fresh-fallen snow near Minnehaha Creek

In time when New York City called
I took flight from home

eked out a living with an Olivetti
read beat poetry by candlelight

Young and light feathered
I set sail on the Atlantic

landing in countries far-off
finding shelter

Later years   along in song
with my love   my matched mate

I crossed mountains and deserts, glided
rivers, oceans, and lakes

guided our young to know new worlds

seeing again through starry eyes

Once more at home but not at rest   a decade
caring for my beloved in decline

I sit now nestled in a chair at my desk
my computer and all the world it brings to me

I reach the crammed bookshelf
at the wall to my left   the top shelf holding

books that I have published   explorers Columbus
and Magellan, Emma Lazarus and the Statue of Liberty…

in moments of reverie I gaze right to a window picture
stone pine trees, squirrels scampering up their branches

I hear a family of crows cawing in quarrel or agreement
they know not one day from another   as I, sheltered here

tap tap tapping on my keyboard, having drifted
from biography to poetic realm

wings at my side   yet poetry is lifting me
slowly   I   rise

Jennifer A. Minotti

FAMILY PHOTO

In the framed 8 1/2 x 11 photo that sat on our player piano for the entirety of my childhood, we are standing under an old apple tree. Mom, dad, and three girls. I am two. My sisters are six and nine. My father is holding me. My middle sister has her arms wrapped so tightly around my father's thigh, it's as if she foresees the impending doom and yearns to hold on to this moment for as long as possible. It is 1971. My dad is a young lawyer. My mother is a stay-at-home mom, cooking hamburgers halfheartedly.

Over decades, I searched for signs in that picture for cracks, foreboding. But the image was persuasive. In those days, success was the three-bedroom house in the leafy suburbs with the kids playing in the front yard and the good school system a mile away. It was a far cry from my parents' own humble upbringings in Washington Heights and tenement housing on the Lower East Side. They had made it.

Soon after this photo was taken—I don't know exactly when—my father began a several-year affair with a woman my parents knew from politics. I was only five or six at the time, but I remember people calling the house at dinnertime to tell my mom that my dad was cheating. Anonymous letters also came to the house—ones my mother rubber-banded and saved in the bottom drawer of her desk.

One night, still holding the yellow rotary phone that was attached to the kitchen wall by its long, tangled cord, I remember my mother yelling, "Mike, you tell these people to stop calling our house!"

But my mom never left, choosing instead to believe the photo on the piano, not the phone calls, letters or actual affair.

Until one day, in 1975, I came home from kindergarten to find my mom shoving my dad's clothes into large, green trash bags. I remember thinking that they used these same green garbage bags not long ago—on Halloween night—to dress up as bags of leaves to go to a party. I was envious at the time that they would be having so much fun without us.

I'll never know what happened on this particular day to make her crack, but she did. With me in tow, my mother got into her light blue station wagon and drove to my dad's office. His beige Mercedes, a symbol of achievement in those days, was parked in the back of the building he owned. As I sat in the front seat of the car, I watched as my mom pulled the garbage bags, one by one, from our back seat and tossed them into the backseat of my dad's car. It's an image I'll never forget.

For another 30 years, that picture remained on my mother's player piano, abandoned like her. Each time I went home—less and less I'll admit—I would stare at that photo. Still searching for evidence of what went wrong. But never finding it.

Since then, I've come to realize two things:

First—Sometimes, you simply don't see it coming.

And second—No matter how many times you scrutinize the past, some things will just never make sense.

Kelly Easton

WHO AM I TODAY?

The hermit or the hermitage. The closed door. The clock. I am the thin space where the breeze comes through the curtains. A hummed melody remembered by no one. I am a labyrinth, a porcupine, a bird of paradise. I am the rusty faucet and the clear water flowing through.

Who am I? I am radical acceptance since control opens doors only unto walls. The emptiness of my own unbelonging. Last night I was invisible, the sheets across my skin like wings. Today I am my work. Have always known that passionate work is the yellow brick road. I am Gramma! And Mom mom mom. Holder of space and hands. A ladle. An open heart.

I am the crone and the hag. The high vibration of my own exuberance, which I tamp down not to be the forceful one, the quirk, the loud mouthed wit. And then, at day's end, I am the home, constantly remodeled, but always with windows, music, and bright and many colors.

Sylvia Alberta

WHO AM I TODAY?

Who am I today?
My failures?
My mental illness?
Am I the sum of
All my broken parts?
My inner selves?

A cloak of an impenetrable and sorrowful fog
Hangs around the inner child's adolescent neck.
She waits in silence ...
Frozen in time
Just as she did
When her innocence and body
Were stolen from her so
Many early morning hours before the sun rose.
She waits for forgiveness.

The shame ebbs and flows
With the tides,
Cresting over rugged cliffs
Spraying sea salt over invisible wounds.

Her adult self walks
As if in a fog ...
When she looks in the mirror,
Her vision is blurred.
Words of compassion
Sound as if she is underwater ...
Faint, muffled.

"Why?" she screams into the wind
Filled with shame and guilt
"Why, did I freeze?"
"Is this who I am today?"

Crystal James

WHO AM I TODAY?

Today, I am a breath of fresh air. Last month marked a year of Trauma Therapy work. I've made tremendous progress yet most of the time, I still feel stuck on the dirt roads I marched on as a child. I walked barefoot down those dirt roads, avoiding sharp rocks and caking my feet in the spray they used as dust control. Just like my aching stained feet, I too feel caked in my traumatic childhood.

In the neighborhood, a stench lingered on hot summer days. The air felt heavy as I tried to avoid the reek. It was the same tactic I used to tiptoe past my passed out alcoholic father. I'd hold my breath until it was safe to breathe. I spent most of my childhood, taking small breaths in and out, to avoid being seen and heard. In one breath, I could walk down my street and past the lined pine grove towards my favorite spot.

Somedays, I feel like I'm still sitting in the White Pine Tree, lovingly named, "The Big Tree." It was a tree I climbed to hide in. To see everything from a bird's eye view. I'd shimmy up the Big Tree, ignoring sap wiped on my forearm even though I'd known it'd be stuck to my arm for days. I'd reach and stretch my tiny body to make it to the tippy top so I could fill my lungs with fresh air. Not the air that seeped out of the rundown trailers and cabins that lined the mucky river. I needed to climb high in search of fresh, clean air.

This week in therapy, I released a story from my pierced lips. A story that isn't my full story but a piece of the rotted pie. I made connections to why I'm always worried that I won't be believed. It's a core belief that I was fed as a child and reinforced time and time again. Now it seeps into my daily life. I'm worried when I call the furniture store to complain that the bed they sold me had an imperfection from delivery that they won't believe anything I say. I'm worried my husband won't believe me when I'm in pain so I lie on the bathroom floor with a burst appendix for far too long. I'm worried my children won't believe me when I tell them I'm sorry for getting too agitated in the morning hours.

As I released stories that reinforced why I don't feel believed, I looked my therapist in her eyes. Waiting. Waiting to see a flash of disbelief. I pride myself on reading moments in glances with people. I look for distrust. However, nothing out of the ordinary happened. Her hazel colored eyes are always patient as I stumble my thoughts and string words together. I felt safe as I looked in her eyes just as I did in the arms of the sturdy Big Tree.

I felt believed.

As I made eye contact, I took a deep breath. It was the same breath I take day after day except oxygen kept filling my lungs like a balloon. Expanding further and further. I took a second deep breath and noticed that it wasn't a fluke. I have a new kind of breath. I've spent this entire week, pausing just to breathe in. It feels new each time. It feels overwhelming knowing that I've been walking around barely breathing my entire life. So today, I can breathe as fresh and clean as when I climbed The Big Tree as a child.

Courtney Glover

WHO AM I TODAY?

Who am I? I often wonder ...
I am a mother and grandmother.
Of that I am certain, but what else?
I am simply a woman, yet so much more.
I am a Christian, trying my best every day.
And far from perfect, without a doubt.
I am overly critical of myself, with self-esteem issues.
I am most certainly my own worst enemy.
I am a sufferer of anxiety and depression.
I am a survivor of abuse, both mental and physical.
I am a poet and a writer, an amateur photographer as well.
But who am I today? I'm still trying to figure that out.
And who I am today is certainly not who I was yesterday.
For better or worse, I'm just me.

Donna Kmetz

A TALE OF TWO MOTHERS

On one hand I have
A presence which smothers
"I love you", "Sweet angels"
Craves attention from others

It confuses and tricks me
My tale of two mothers

Then there's biology
A choice not to stay
Parent and daughter
She kept me at bay

One's way to nurture
Is saccharine sweet
Tastes good at the onset
The aftertaste's beat

The other is harder
To get a bead on
There's no real connection
Discomfort is strong

Two maternal figures
Two sides of a coin
The differences blatant
Which side would I join

Where would I land
On the spectrum of care
Would I know how to love
Or, like them, would I err

Will my son understand
My limitations and flaws
Will my instincts kick in
Will I stop and give pause?

In this grand scheme of life,
Intertwined with each other
We live and we learn
My tale of three mothers.

Áine Greaney

A FAITHFUL HEART

Today I am sitting on the sea wall watching four swans and watching the hours and minutes until it's time to drive my husband to the hospital for outpatient surgery.

A new swan glides into view. Now they are five.

Today will be the fifth hospital trip.

Mostly I remember silly things, like that ER waiting room where none of us met each other's eyes. Or that snack machine where the potato chips jammed and I body slammed it to release a food I don't like. An office where I did my day job work with the cell phone set on high. When it rang, it was not the surgeon, but someone calling across state lines because, she said, she hated to wait for these things.

I wanted to tell her this: Good waiting makes a good hospital.

Books I've read. Pages I've written. Deadlines I've met because it's amazing what you can do while the machines bleep and the patients sleep and you keep busy because, really, nobody wants to deal with a bothersome wife.

New swans have arrived. Now they are nine.

There's an old ballad about a swan. I remember it now: It's that one about how swans mate for life, and—oh, yes—there's a line about the male swan's "faithful heart."

Sitting here on the sea wall I think: Easy for the bloody swans.

Sitting here on the sea wall I ask: Who the heck gets to define 'faithful?'

Sitting here on the sea wall I think how, once, I thought I could list the component parts (of a faithful heart).

As I leave the sea wall, I think how, some days, faithfulness is a to-do list that gets done; this thing and then this next thing, one by one.

Anjana Deshpande

SPELL

"Take a piece of paper, rip its edges
We need it to be flowing, natural
No hard lines"
Said the woman in the video
On how to bring back a lost love.

She took her time
explaining simple tasks
like choosing the right pen,
the right color.
How to boldly write the
Name
of the one who has forgotten you,
and then fold the piece of paper
just so.

Crisp lines closing over the name
like a fist.
Keep it under the pillow for three moons,
then burn it.

Scatter the ashes,

and you will be remembered.

That night, I took a piece of paper
and wrote
my name.

Rose Loving

WHO AM I TODAY?

I go outside and the door to my world swings open. It appears spring has truly arrived. The deck furniture stacked in the garage is begging for fresh air. I imagine hauling it out and head to the tool bucket for gloves. The corner of my eye catches sight of the Mellow Yellow Spiraea and I stop to pick leaves and scratch the dirt around it. I glance at the Barberry on the nearby bank and stoop to clean it out. Then I remember the nasty thorns. They are so tiny and insignificant for days until they fester in the fingers, hard to find, but easy to feel.

Surfacing from my reverie, I recall the journey to the gloves. I find myself, at the pea row, thinking of the clasp leaf hands inside each shell, quietly listening for that subtle drum beat. The rhythmic call to break free. While turning the dark musky soil, I wonder what else resides in this fertile bed before nestling the peas into place. I shed my earthly layer for a moment to look up and catch the red swollen buds atop the maples. Soon the spring green will roll up the valley. Dark shadows stretch across the hills conversing with the light unfolding behind clouds.

Both ominous and illuminating, a scale to balance the weather to come. I am upward now like the cupped branches of the Ginko waiting for the rain to broaden its reach and open its palms. Finally, I free a chair from the garage, place it on the deck and take the seat. I think about tea but have a few breaths instead to ponder this moment.

What I know today is that I am all of this. I am the door swinging open. I am the thorns that fester when I encounter my own irritation at my human race. I am the dark shadows as well as the light behind them. The pressed hands in the pea seeds trusting when to cast off the unneeded shell and break new ground. The nourishing rain we know will arrive, cold as it might be, but warmly welcomed. I am all of this. Today I am all these things because today I have the eyes to see we are all the same.

Sarah Birnbach

AWAKENING

I am seven plus decades, a septuagenarian who realizes daily that more of my life is behind me than in front of me, and so

I am a woman who cherishes every day, looking for the beauty and goodness in everything and everyone around me.

I am a woman who takes the time to delight in the giggles of children, the sounds, sights, and smells of the ocean, the colors of nature, the magnitude of sunsets.

I am a woman who understands the importance of relationships, who takes time to nurture them,

who never hesitates to say "I love you" to those who mean the most to me, and who says "I'm sorry" when I behave less than I would have liked.

I am Jewish and no longer afraid to speak it out loud, no longer cowering under the fear of anti-Semites who would wish me dead, feeling braver and stronger than I have ever been before.

I am the bearer of arthritic knees who struggles to stand up after playing on the floor with my grandsons but who can still bench press 45 pounds in the gym and lift my 30-pound grandson and play soccer with his brother and feel proud that I can.

I am a woman who carries the scars of a heart broken by a daughter who chose to cut off from my love without explanation. But like the Japanese art of Kintsugi, I have mended that crack with the gold of my positive memories.

I am a woman proud of every silver sparkle on my scalp that some would call gray hair but which I prefer to honor as witnesses to my life's journey.

I am a woman committed to doing the right thing for the right reason regardless of the costs in time, energy, and emotional stamina.

I am a woman who holds onto optimism, integrity, and principles in the face of others' prejudices, divisiveness, and moral failings and feel shameless pride in doing so.

I am a woman who has learned to conquer fear and use my voice and my pen to educate others and fight for social justice.

I am a woman grateful to the Almighty for the many blessings that have enhanced my life.

Who am I today? I am the best version of myself that I have ever been.

Marjorie Moorhead

WHO AM I TODAY?

Today,
I am writing; I am a writer.
I am listening.
I am a mother.
A daughter; a birdwatcher.
An owl. Mourning dove. The clouds,
full Pink Super Moon, and more.
I am all of the above.
And below, I am the roots
the dirt the leaves decaying.
Do you know the term "mycelial"?
How lovely the web of an organic extending
reaching arms finding all, enabling life
and survival. I am a part of that network too.
Grains of dirt; the water flowing through;
the minerals feeding seeds and bulbs. Yes.
And I am the sunset, pink-orange and going down.
I am a pine tree grown tall. I am a far-away star
twinkling, always around, but truly seen
only when the dark is deep enough.
I am a mountain; blue and majestic. Come,
soar with me today as we sail into magnificence!

AUTHOR BIOGRAPHIES

Amy Agigian is Associate Professor in the Sociology and Criminal Justice department at Suffolk University and founding director of the Center for Women's Health and Human Rights. She is honored and thrilled to be pursuing her feminist dreams as Executive Director of Our Bodies Ourselves Today (ourbodiesourselvestoday.org).

Sylvia Alberta has had a fulfilling career in education for 30+ years. She is a wife and proud mom of two sons. Sylvia is a middle-plus aged woman working through her PTSD/TRAUMA which goes back decades. She is slogging and slushing in the muck to find peace, hope and a more mindful path.

Dipti B is an MA Sociology student from Nepal. She uses paints and brushes to raise voices against mental illness and women's violence. Her artwork is on Instagram @the_birdy_arts. Her artwork and prose have appeared in Beyond Words International Literary Magazine, Polemicalzine, Wearezanna, Journal of Expressive Writing, and The Brooklyn Review.

Sarah Birnbach began her encore career as a nonfiction writer after careers as a management consultant, motivational speaker, and family therapist. Sarah's lifelong journaling practice informs her writing, for which she has received multiple awards and publications. Her memoir, *A Daughter's Kaddish: My Year of Grief, Devotion, and Healing*, was published in September 2022.

Raluca Buttner has always found great happiness in any creative outlet—writing being one of her favorites—since she was little. She writes for herself, and occasionally to share with others, and hopes to continue creating for the rest of her life.

Joni B. Cole is the author of six books, including the writing guide, *Good Naked: How to Write More, Write Better, and Be Happier* (listed as one of the "Best Books for Writers," by Poets & Writers). Joni is also the creator/host of the podcast *Author, Can I Ask You?* More at: jonibcole.com

Abha Das Sarma is an engineer and management consultant by profession, but enjoys writing the most. Besides having a blog of over 200 poems (dassarmafamily.blogspot.com), her poems have appeared in Muddy River Poetry Review, Spillwords, Verse-Virtual, Visual Verse, The Ekphrastic Review, and Journal of Expressive Writing among others.

Anjana Deshpande is a published poet, poetry therapist, teacher, and licensed clinician. Originally from India, Anjana has been in the US for over 20 years. As a Certified Journal and Poetry Therapist, Anjana incorporates her love for words in her work with mental illness, and is the founder of writethought.org.

Melanie Devoid is a retired educator. She loves reading, writing and learning. She started writing as a therapeutic way of dealing with traumatic events. Melanie continues to write to encourage and inspire others by sharing her stories of perseverance, faith and hope.

Debra Dolan lives in the beautiful seaside walkable community of Ambleside, West Vancouver in Canada. She is a self-described pluviophile, avid reader of women's memoir, and private journaller for over 50 years. Debra enjoys enlightening conversations over red wine, solo nature hikes, and traveling. Her writings have appeared in numerous North American publications.

Amy Donahue is a technologist and a creator. She lives south of Boston with her husband and three children.

Kelly Easton is a mental health counselor, teacher, and writer. She lives in beautiful Marblehead, MA, and Sarasota, FL, so she can swim in the ocean every day of the year with her husband, children, and grandchildren.

Lisa Friedlander is a psychotherapist and essayist who loves to quilt together experiences, ideas, characters, reflections, and sensory details. Recent works appear in Shark Reef, apo*press, Ponder Review, Wild Roof, Adanna Literary Review, Pink Panther, and Epiphany.

Audrey Geliga graduated from St. John's University. She worked in television before she decided to be a stay at home mom. She has two children, both of whom have Special Needs. She spent years advocating through children's books, a blog, public speaking workshops, and having a book club of her own.

Courtney Glover is originally from Fulton County, Georgia. She is a writer, published author, editor, and amateur photographer. She is the author of four poetry books, including

Calypso Dreaming: A Collection of Poetry. She is also the editor of *The Sacred Feminine: An Open Skies Collection* anthology and the *Open Skies Poetry* anthology.

Áine Greaney is an Irish-born author who lives and writes on Boston's North Shore. In addition to her five books, her essays and stories have appeared in publications such as Creative Nonfiction, The Boston Globe Magazine and The World Channel. She teaches writing to community groups. More at: ainegreaney.com

Paula Hagar lives and writes in Denver, Colorado. She has been an avid journal writer for 55 years. Her passions are traveling the U.S. entirely on back roads while writing, photographing and painting her adventures. She has been published in several anthologies. Her mantra is "wander often, wonder always."

Taslim Jaffer is currently working on her debut memoir-in-essays which is a multi-generational saga of migration, culture and identity. She is a mom of three kids and a dog, a writing instructor, and a freelance editor. Taslim holds an MFA in Creative Nonfiction from the University of King's College in Halifax, NS.

Crystal James is a writer, poet, and artist. She believes in the power of being vulnerable with an open heart. This honest approach allows for healing with hopes of helping others along the way. Her writing is published in the Kindred Voice, Journal of Expressive Writing, and Motherscope.

Donna Kmetz is a transplanted Jersey girl living on the Florida gulf coast. Professionally, as *The Freckled Beachcomber*, she refinished furniture combining coastal flair with an upcycled conscience. Personally, she is an emotional ball of feelings funneling from her heart to her fingers using the written word as a therapeutic outlet.

Noelle Lee is a graduate of Boston University (B.A.) and University of Pennsylvania (M.S.Ed.) and has passions for expressive writing, journaling, comparative religious studies in Christianity and Judaism, and fine art.

Terri Lee is a multidisciplinary designer living in Rochester, NY where she immigrated at the age of seven months. She reconnected with her Korean heritage living in South Korea for two years, but it wasn't until the world shut down for COVID that she began to reflect on her identity as a Korean American.

Barrie Levine practiced family law in Massachusetts, dedicated to representing women, from 1973 to 2016. She began writing haiku poetry in her seventies, an incredibly generative decade. She also writes a blog, *"72 is the New 72"* at barrielevine.com and recently published a collection of 127 haiku entitled *COTTON MOON*.

Nancy Smiler Levinson is author of *MOMENTS OF DAWN: A Poetic Memoir of Love & Family, Affliction & Affirmation*, as well as 30 books for young readers. Her work has appeared in numerous journals and anthologies, most recently Global Poemic, Sleet, Writing in a Woman's Voice, Journal of Expressive Writing, and the Jewish Literary Journal.

Rose Loving moved to Vermont 47 years ago and knew that it was home. She graduated from Johnson State College, where she found a passion for ceramics. Rose has worked as a public school teacher, managed a gardening business, and taught yoga. Always a journaler, recently her focus is creative writing and poetry.

Marjorie Moorhead originally found her voice in poetry through examining a long, formative survival journey. Her poems are collected in the chapbooks, *Survival: Trees, Tides, Song* (FLP, 2019), and *Survival Part 2: Trees, Birds, Ocean, Bees* (Duck Lake Books, 2020), as well as a variety of anthologies and journals.

Deirdre Maher is a writer and poet. A number of her stories and poems appear in various anthologies, online and in print. She completed an MA in Creative Writing at the University of Kingston, London in September 2020, with Distinction. Deirdre lives in London and is happiest when writing. More at: @dmar_miss

Julie Johnson McVeigh is a friend who is learning to listen for when she is hungry, eat, write, and do. She hears a voice for what is true. Here, she finds her companion. She is funny and smart and enough to be the friend where she calls home.

Jennifer A. Minotti is a Writer-in-Residence at the Center for Women's Health and Human Rights at Suffolk University. Founder of the Women's Writing Circle and the Journal of Expressive Writing, Jen co-created The World's Very First Gratitude Parade and helped establish Gratitude Day in Cambridge, MA.

Jyoti Nair is intrigued with the human behavior spectrum, its layered richness, and uncanny complexities. Her works have found havens in the anthologies *The Kali Project & Through The Looking Glass,* Open Skies Quarterly, Impspired, Lothlorien Poetry Journal, Journal of Expressive Writing, Indian Periodical, The Times Group Femina, Delhi Post, and other journals.

Jessie North has worked over many years in the literary arts on projects from website marketing to children's plays. Following a spinal cord injury and soulful introspection, she now feels free to share from her most inner self and in her own voice. Jessie and her family live in New Hampshire.

Adeola Sheehy is an Irish/Nigerian Londoner now living in the New Forest, with her four home educated children. Writing from the crossroads of race, womanhood, and creativity she uses prose to tackle the questions her mind ponders most and poetry to express the feelings closest to her heart.

Barbara Simmons is a native Bostonian residing in California, Wellesley College graduate, and retired teacher and counselor. She explores the communion of words as ways to remember and envision. Publications include Boston Accent, NewVerse News, Soul-Lit, and Capsule Stories (Autumn & Winter, 2020). *Offertories: Exclamations and Disequilibriums* is her first book of poetry (Spring, 2022).

Noelle Sterne is an author, editor, and mentor who has published over 700 essays, stories, writing craft articles, spiritual pieces, and poems. She authored *Challenges in Writing Your Dissertation: Coping with the Emotional, Interpersonal, and*

Spiritual Struggles and *Trust Your Life: Forgive Yourself and Go After Your Dreams*. More at: trustyourlifenow.com

Jyotirmaya Thakur is a retired Principal and author of more than 40 books. She is a multigenre award winning poet, book reviewer, translator, columnist, social and environmental activist, and healer. Her work has been published in global anthologies, magazines, tabloids, and digital news-media and has been translated into many languages.

Renu Sarah Thomas is a BAAT registered Art Psychotherapist, educator and workshop facilitator. Born in India, she has spent her growing years in England, Nigeria and Saudi Arabia and currently lives in Dubai (UAE). She is a self-taught artist who passionately encourages others to pursue some form of creative expression.

Donna Truong is a graduate of UMASS Lowell and currently works in the medical device industry. She is also the creator and podcast host of *What Even Is...?* where she fulfills her desire to learn more about random topics by interviewing experts. Additionally, she is an ordained minister.

Andrea Twombly, a Native New Englander, is a retired manufacturing business owner who adores words and has abandoned number-filled days with glee. An author by surprise, she has published five Christmas stories and one novel. She is a mother of one and grandmother of one. Andrea will love and miss her late husband forever.

Christine "Cissy" White is a joy-stalking writer with ovarian cancer and PTSD. She's been published in Ms. Magazine, The Boston Globe, and The Elephant Journal. Her advocacy has been highlighted in The Boston Globe, Atlantic Monthly, and on PBS NewsHour. She lives in MA and blogs at Heal Write Now (healwritenow.com).

Cigeng Zhang is a freelance English translator from China. She began writing poems in English in 2012. Her several poems were included in The Poetic Bond series (published in the UK) from 2013 to 2020. *Rouge in the Water* was her first bilingual collection of poems published in China in 2017.

ACKNOWLEDGMENTS

aka Gratitudes

I am forever grateful to each writer in this anthology who trusted me with their writing. I know how precious their voices are and I do not take that privilege lightly.

I want to thank the hundreds of women who have attended my Women's Writing Circles over the years. I am humbled, inspired and uplifted by your courage and by your words. Do not stop writing and sharing your voice. Your words matter. YOU matter.

I also wish to thank the women who supported me in the years preceding this anthology. Each has a hand in this publication whether they realize it or not. They include:

Joni Cole, who facilitated the very first Women's Writing Circle when I was too scared to do so myself, and when I needed to be a participant the most.

Nancy Aronie who encouraged me to write from my grieving heart.

Cissy White, whose constant support, love, and encouragement gave me the courage to facilitate my very first Circle.

Deborah Sosin, Leslie Laurence and Kathleen Adams who

provided compassionate spaces for me to write my truths.

Amy Agigian for giving the Women's Writing Circle a home within the Center for Women's Health and Human Rights at Suffolk University.

Judith Zorfass, my first mentor whose strong work ethic taught me to always strive to produce the highest quality work in every project and task.

In addition:

It is impossible to speak when you are muted. I want to thank the many women in my life who have not silenced me. You know who you are. To those who tried, but were unsuccessful, I thank you for being my greatest teachers.

To my mother and grandmother, thank you for modeling strength, devotion and love.

To Tod, Zeno, Sola, and LuLu. I love you more.

And finally, to everyone reading this anthology. Writers need readers and women's voices need to be heard. Thank you for holding these 40 women's stories with such tenderness and care.

ABOUT THE EDITOR

For the past 25 years, **Jennifer A. Minotti** has dedicated her professional life towards working for the betterment of society. She considers her life's mission to be one where she can help to improve, transform and support the lives of others. Currently, she is accomplishing this through the use of expressive writing, authentic listening, respect for all voices, and an ongoing commitment to diversity, equity, inclusion, social justice, and anti-racism/anti-bias. Jen considers herself a relationship-builder, inclusive community weaver, social and racial justice advocate, narrative change-maker, and life-long gratitude apprentice.

Since 2015, Jen has been Writer-in-Residence at the Center for Women's Health and Human Rights at Suffolk University in Boston, MA. In 2020, Jen founded the Journal of Expressive Writing in order to provide a place for sharing expressive writing, believing that we need this space on a fundamental, human level and that whatever we are feeling is a link to what others are feeling across the planet at any given moment. For 17 years prior to founding the Women's Writing Circle and the Journal of Expressive Writing, Jen worked at Education Development Center (EDC)—a global non-profit working to improve education, health, and economic opportunities worldwide—in a variety of writing, research, technology, teaching, and leadership roles.

Jen is a graduate of Boston University (B.S.) and Columbia University (M.A., M.Ed) and is a Certified Journal to the Self Instructor. Her writing and poetry can be found in refereed journals, literary publications, and anthologies. Jen lives in Cambridge, MA with her husband and children.

LEARN MORE AT:

womenswritingcircle.com
journalofexpressivewriting.com

CPSIA information can be obtained
at www.ICGtesting.com
Printed in the USA
BVHW040806050323
659706BV00018B/905